God's Faithful Servant:
The Story of Old Regular Baptist Preacher I.D. Back

Kristi Dixon

God's Faithful Servant:
The Story of Old Regular Baptist Preacher I.D. Back

Copyright 2006 Kristi Dixon
All Rights Reserved
ISBN: 978-0-6151-4197-8
Front Cover Photo: Gravesite of I.D. and Ina Rose Back
Back Page Photo: Picture of the Author
Formatting: David Chaltas

DEDICATION

In conducting research to prepare for the writing of this book, I have spent countless hours talking with friends and family members of Elder I.D. Back. In January 2001, I was even privileged enough to have the opportunity to interview the man himself.

The day was very cold. The remains of what had been a significant snowfall remained on his sloped lawn. Despite the cold temperatures and the presence of lingering snow, however, the sun was shining brightly on this particular Saturday afternoon, and, when I went to I.D.'s home, his mood was as bright as the shining sun. That is to say, he was in good spirits.

After approaching his house, I knocked on the door. At that point, I heard a cheerful voice yell, "Tony! Tony! Heyyyyyyyyyyyy, Tony!" I.D., who was bedfast and could not come answer the door for himself, was calling out for his younger son Tony, who was caring for him on this particular day, to come and do so.

When Tony heard his father's voice and opened the door to welcome me into the Back home, I entered the kitchen and then walked into the living room. Only the sun shining through the window, next to the hospital bed in which the frail, little body was resting, served to light this room. The bed was positioned in such a manner as to allow him to view, through a large picture window, cars passing on the road that ran past the lower part of his property.

I commented on how well he looked on this particular day. Cheerfully, he replied that Tony had cleaned him up. He was excited about the prospect of this book. The inflections that were evident in his voice, as I later played back a taped recording of our conversation, lent support to the notion that he was greatly enjoying this opportunity to tell about days gone by. During the course of the interview, we were briefly interrupted when Tony came into the room and began joking with his father. After a few moments of tolerance, the father jokingly said to the son that it was time for him to leave the room now, because, "We're talking turkey!" He wanted to keep sharing with this author those memories that were so precious to him, and he wouldn't tolerate interruption...even from his beloved son!

Later that evening, long after I had left the Back home and ventured on to other destinations, my father spoke with I.D. on the phone. Dad later commented that I.D. had been so excited after my visit. For that, I am thankful. He gave so much to others during his lifetime. If I was able to bring him just a little happiness by sitting and listening to his remembrance of precious moments in his life, then I am so happy that I was able to do that much for him.

I obtained a lot of interesting information on that day; however, I needed to ask him several more questions at some point, and, as I left, I told him that I would return on another day and have him tell me more. He had been ill, after all, and I did not want to tire him. Sadly, however, that was to be the last time that I visited with I.D. Back.

Shortly after that visit, he sustained injuries in a fall from his bed, as he tried, presumably, to rise from bed and answer the ringing telephone. He was admitted to the hospital once again, at that point, and then he was moved to a nursing home, where he died after only a very brief stay.

As I was never able to interview him again, I had to reconstruct much of his life story via information obtained from other sources. Needed information was obtained via interviews with his family and friends, the reading of his journal entries, the reading of books and articles written by others, and interviews conducted by others and accessed to me by family members. I also called upon my own experiences with, and personal observations of, this man during the years that I was privileged to know him. With reliance on information from all of these sources, I am attempting, in this book, to elaborate upon the life and times of one of the greatest mortal men to ever walk upon this earth. It is to the memory of this man, I.D. Back, that I dedicate this book.

I.D. Back
(Personal collection of Elwood Cornett)

FOREWARD

There is a scripture, in the Holy Bible, which instructs us to give honor where honor is due (Romans 13:7). In 1st Timothy (5:17), it is stated that we should "Let the elders that rule well be counted worthy of double honor, especially they who labor in the word and doctrine." The Bible further states, "And every one that hath forsaken houses, or brethren, or sisters, or father, or mother, or wife, or children, or lands, for my name's sake, shall receive an hundredfold, and shall inherit everlasting life" (Matthew 19:29). I can think of no man existing during the course of my lifetime who better heeded that latter directive from the Bible, or more fully met the qualifications of those to whom honor is due, than did the late Old Regular Baptist preacher, I.D. Back.

The reader will note that, throughout the course of this book, I.D. is never referred to as "Reverend." This is in keeping with the teachings of the Old Regular Baptists. Elder Elwood Cornett, moderator of the Indian Bottom Association of the Old Regular Baptists, states that, in reference to one who preaches God's Word, the word "Reverend" is not used in the Holy Bible. My father, Elder Danny Dixon, referred me to the one scripture in the Bible in which reverend is used. That scripture states, "He sent redemption unto His people: He hath commanded His covenant forever: holy and reverend is His name" (Psalms 111:9). This latter scripture indicates, according to the teachings in the Old Regular Baptist Church, that only God is to be referred to as "Reverend."

Elder Cornett states that referring to a preacher as a reverend might give the appearance of bestowing undue greatness upon a mere man. The word "Reverend," he says, would indicate that a man is revered. As stated above, it is the belief of Old Regular Baptists that only God, and not man, is to be revered. Thus, Elder Cornett has stated that those who preach the gospel in the Old Regular Baptist churches would never want to be referred to as "Reverend." They would prefer, instead, to be referred to as "preachers" or "elders."

According to those who knew him well, this was definitely true of Elder I.D. Back. Thus, out of respect for this belief, the author will make reference in this book to "preachers," "ministers," and "elders."

During the time that I have spent conducting research for this book, no one has been able to tell me exactly how many funerals Elder I.D. Back preached during his 75 years on earth. None, however, have hesitated to estimate the number to be in the thousands. When his death was reported in his native Letcher County's newspaper, *The Mountain Eagle*, the newspaper article indicated that there were times when he preached as many as 85 funeral services in one year. Elder Elwood Cornett recalls being told by I.D. that Walton Back (a brother who preceded him in death) once kept count of the number of funerals he preached in a particular year. Elder Cornett did not know what the final count was for that year, but he did know that the number had surpassed 100 by the month of October.

For years, one could listen to the obituary column presented via a local radio station and hear the name of I.D. Back (as one of the given funeral's officiating ministers) numerous times daily. I.D.'s son Ronald "Ronnie" Back would recall in years after his father's death that, upon I.D.'s "passing," it took him some time to come to terms with the fact that he could no longer learn of his father's whereabouts on a particular day simply by listening to the obituary column. This son remembers that, in months following I.D.'s death, he would be driving down the road and start to turn the radio on and listen to the obituaries, before remembering that he would no longer be able to hear his father's name listed as one of the preachers participating in the funeral services discussed.

In addition to the numerous funerals that he preached in his lifetime, Elder I.D. Back performed countless wedding ceremonies and baptisms, preached innumerable church services, and visited hordes of sick, lonely, and mourning individuals and families. In reading through the journals that he wrote in daily during some of his latter years, I noted that entries were short. I suspect that this was due in part to fatigue and failing health. I further suspect, however, that this was due to lack of time, as he was busy performing the Lord's work throughout much of the day. More important than the length of the entries, however, was the content. In days when he was still able to travel, his entries focused largely upon the sick that he had visited that day or the people in his network of friends and acquaintances who had recently succumbed to death.

Ronnie Back has recalled that his father's fixation upon death and dying became a bit irritating to family members in latter years. As so much of Elder Back's conversations were centered around these topics, family members thought that he was being morbid. In fact, though, he was simply talking about the topics that were a central part of his daily life.

As a child, I knew that I.D. Back was loved and respected. I can recall seeing him preaching on the church stand during Sunday morning services, and then, while still preaching his sermons, leaving the stand and progressing down the aisle to hug and shake hands of members of the congregation. He had a kind word for each of us, old and young alike. "I love you, Honey." "God bless you, Honey." These were sentiments that I heard frequently over the years.

It was not, however, until I became older that I realized just how great of an impact I.D. Back had had upon, not only those in our community, but, people across the country. It was not until the time of his death, which was covered on a local television news program and in, not only our local papers, but also in newspapers as far away as Lexington, Kentucky, how much of a celebrity of sorts this small man from a small town had become.

His death, undoubtedly, came as a major shock to many. We in the community had watched his health deteriorate for years and knew that, as nature dictates, death would soon be upon the horizon. Still, the finality of its actual occurrence struck those who knew and loved I.D. Back (as well as those who just knew of him) with that awful hurt that accompanies the final disappearance of anything good. At this point, community members no longer just talked about how much we would all miss him when he died and how much the Old Regular Baptist churches might suffer as a result of his passing. We now were actually experiencing the awful void that we had long anticipated.

When Elder Back died, visitation services were held for two nights prior to his funeral. His body, of course, would lie in state at his beloved Mt. Olivet Old Regular Baptist Church.

On the first night of visitation, I did not attend services. I had some errands to run, and, by the time I returned from running these errands, it was late, and I certainly did not look presentable enough to attend a visitation service. Still, however, there was a longing inside me to be near the people attending this service. I knew that I.D. had been a great man in life, and I was just yearning to attend his services and offer my last respects. So, while I didn't attend the visitation service that night, I did drive over to the church. In getting to the church, I drove across the same old, blue, steel bridge that I.D.

had so often driven over himself in past years. Sometimes, he would have come across this bridge for the purpose of participating in happy events, such as festivities associated with the annual Blackey Day celebration or the chance to enter the Blackey Senior Citizen Center (the site for voting in the Blackey precinct) and cast his vote for some friend or family member who had ventured to seek political office. On other occasions, though, he had crossed this bridge for the same purpose that I was crossing it on this night...to pay last respects to the dearly departed.

It was quite late, and, as I recall, the temperature on that night was bitterly cold. The remains of a recent snowfall covered portions of the ground. Still, the lights inside the Mount Olivet Old Regular Baptist Church were shining brightly. The porch light was burning outside, and a few of the mourners who still had not left for the night were assembled on the porch, engaging in conversation. As I mentioned, I did not go into the building on this night. Instead, I simply circled around Blackey in my car, passing buildings, houses, and sites that had played such an important role in the life of I.D. Back. Then, I went back across the blue, steel bridge and turned onto Route 7, which would lead me to my residence at Letcher.

As I drove along Route 7, I could look across the river that separates this road from the Mt. Olivet Church in downtown Blackey and see lights burning through the back windows of that old church that I.D. had helped establish so many years earlier and had come to love so dearly over the course of the years. As I drove, I began thinking more about just how much our community was changed with his passing. I realized that I would never have the opportunity to be baptized by I.D. Back, because I had waited too late to seek the salvation that would have allowed me to experience that particular honor. No matter how soon I sought salvation at this point, I would never be able to have I.D. accompany me into the water of the Kentucky River and baptize me.

I had also delayed my own marriage too long. As a child, I would sometimes plan out my future wedding. Plans have never been finalized, as, to date, I remain single. In at least some of these planned wedding ceremonies, though, I am sure that I.D. Back would have been the officiating minister of choice. This would no longer be a possibility.

As my drive progressed, I began to think about the fact that I had, in the past, associated I.D. Back with the death or sickness of a family member or loved one. I had grown up knowing that, if I (or anyone in my family) became ill, we could call I.D. and he would come visit us. He would pray for us. That knowledge was truly comforting, for, just as I am convinced that my own parents have a direct line to Heaven, I was sure that God would hear I.D.'s prayers for us, too. Throughout my life, I had witnessed him visiting homes when friends and family members died. Somehow, he had managed to bring a sense of comfort with him.

I began to think about the fact that life, as I had always known it, would never again be the same. I.D. had now served his time on earth. He was no longer going to be at the beck and call of Kristi Dixon or anyone else on earth that might need his services. He had fought a good fight on earth, performing the work that God had given him to do. Now, his work on earth was finished, and he had gone home to Heaven to receive his final reward. Those of us left on earth would now have to learn to "get through" without him. This was a very saddening thought for me, simply for selfish reasons.

On the second night of visitation services, I made it a point to be in attendance. I arrived late in the service, and the church was filled to capacity. There was standing room only. I was standing at the very back of the building near the double doors through which I had just entered. However uncomfortable this might have been physically, it did give me the opportunity to obtain a large, overall view of the congregation (from behind). Thus, when the preacher asked for a show of hands from all of those whose lives had been touched in some way by I.D. Back, I watched as more than 75% of the congregation's hands were raised in unison with my own. It was a very touching moment. (At a memorial service held at Mt. Olivet Old Regular Baptist Church approximately three months after I.D.'s death, I would see this scene repeated, as groups of people stood when the preacher called for those who I.D. had married, those who he had baptized, those who had called him to preach in the funeral service of a loved one, and those whose lives he had simply "touched" in some way. I feel certain that, at some point, 99-100% of the people in the church stood.)

Later, as people began leaving for the night and the size of the congregation diminished, I moved closer to the front of the church and sat in one of the pews with my aunt, Pat Fields Caudill. From this vantage point, I could clearly see I.D. resting peacefully in his coffin. Pictures of him in his younger years, including at least one, which depicted him in military attire, were assembled on and near the coffin. I was struck by a strong resemblance between a picture of young I.D. Back and his grandson, Anthony. Near the casket, there rested a flower arrangement that had been sent from the old war buddy who had saved his life so many years ago. There were also flowers from many others who had experienced the pleasure of encountering I.D. Back at some point in their lives.

The next day was Friday. I returned to the Mt. Olivet Old Regular Baptist Church for the funeral services. Again, the building was full. The service went smoothly, and I recall feeling sadness as the service ended and the tiny body in the casket was wheeled to the back of the church house to allow one final viewing by the congregation. As I exited the church, I looked into the coffin at the cold, still body. Alas, he was at rest.

After the funeral, my father drove to the cemetery where I.D. was to be buried. I rode along. My parents' 1992 Toyota Camry wound around the old River Road that I.D. had traveled so often throughout the course of his life. Dad parked on the roadside and walked up a hill to a cemetery that could not be viewed from the road. It was there that I.D.'s casket would be lowered into the cool, damp earth. During the burial service, my mother and I had remained in the car, where it was warm and dry. Soon, Dad came back to the car and we departed the area.

I noticed, during our brief journey, that a train was stopped on the tracks. As trains had played such a significant role in I.D.'s life (e.g., carrying him off to serve in World War II, bringing him home from war, providing a depot at which he could court his future wife, and sounding the loud horn that he undoubtedly had heard from his home for so many years), it was fitting that it had stopped. It was as if even the trains knew that a great man had passed from this world and, in particular, from the small community of Blackey, and felt that a moment of stillness and silence should be demonstrated in tribute to his memory.

AUTHOR'S COMMENTS

So many people have been so helpful to me during the time that I spent in writing and seeking publication for this book. It would be a huge task for me to name them all. I.D. Back's family members, his friends, members of the community, and members of the Indian Bottom Association of the Old Regular Baptists graciously provided the author with interviews. They all provided information that was helpful in the creation of this story, and I would like to extend a special, heartfelt thanks to each of those individuals.

I hope that this finished work makes all of you who contributed stories, dates, etc. very proud. If any errors are present, they are unintentional. The author made a good-faith effort to record information as it was reported to her, and she is not to be held liable for any discrepancies.

Ronald Wakefield "Ronnie" Back and Sherry Back Fugate, living children of I.D. Back, have been so helpful in providing family documents, pictures, tapes, and stories. They were also kind enough to let me borrow and read journals that I.D. kept throughout some of the latter years of his life. The creation of this book has been a long process, and I would like to extend a special thanks to Ronnie and Sherry for their patience.

I also extend a special thanks to Old Regular Baptist preacher Elwood Cornett. As a lifelong friend of the Back family, Elder Cornett was an endless source of information. He graciously took time out of his busy schedule to review the draft of this book and ensure that, to the best of his knowledge, this author had stated all facts correctly.

Another special thanks is extended to L.M. "Mike" Caudill. A native Letcher Countian who pursued a career in law before being named CEO to the Mountain Comp. Health Care Center, Mr. Caudill was kind enough to prepare the legal release used in order to get permission to publish information provided by those interviewed for this book.

Yet another special thanks goes out to author David "Butch" Chaltas. Without his help in "learning the ropes" about publication, I would have been lost! Not only did he loan me a book about publication and suggest a publishing company that would do quality work, but he was kind enough to take the time to help me get the book into a format that would be acceptable to a publishing company. (Shannon Smith also offered advice regarding publication, and is greatly appreciated.)

I reserve a huge thanks for my parents, Danny and Teresa Fields Dixon. My father was the person who originally suggested that I write a book about I.D. Back. He was also the person who first called I.D. and asked him if he would be willing to let me write a book about his life. At times when I started "slacking" and not working on the book as diligently as I should have, my parents were the people who reminded me that I needed to work harder and get this book completed as quickly as possible. They have always been there for me (as well as for my sister, Misti), offering love, support, and encouragement, and I thank them for this.

The greatest thanks, however, should be extended to God. Without His help, I would not have been able to even lift my fingers to type the words that are on these pages. Without God, I.D. Back would not have become a man worthy of being written about in a book. Without God, those reading this book would not have the ability to read. Without Him, none of us would even be in existence. Hence, it is to Him that the greatest amount of thanks is due.

ABOUT THE AUTHOR

Kristi Dixon was born and raised in the mountains of Southeastern Kentucky. In 1976, when Kristi was four-years-old, her mother and father joined the Cedar Grove Old Regular Baptist Church. Kristi has regularly attended Old Regular Baptist church services since that time. She is a 1990 graduate of Letcher High School. She obtained a Bachelor's of Science Degree in the area of communication disorders from Eastern Kentucky University in December 1993. Also from Eastern Kentucky University, she earned a Master's Degree in Communication Disorders (1995) and a Rank I in Special Education (1997). Since January 1996, she has been employed by the Letcher County Board of Education as a speech-language pathologist. She enjoys writing stories and poetry, reading, and shopping. This is her first novel.

(Author during interview)

TABLE OF CONTENTS

Dedication 3
Foreward 6
Author's Comments 14
About the Author 16

CHAPTER

1 The Town of Blackey 18
2 Genealogy 22
3 Blackey's Newest Citizen 24
4 School Days 27
5 Life at Home 37
6 Military Service 44
7 Working and Playing in Post-War Years 53
8 Courtship and Marriage 57
9 Married…But Not Quite Settled Down 62
10 God Has Mercy on I.D.'s Soul 65
11 Separate Classifications of Old Regular Baptists ... 71
12 A Calling to the Ministry 75
13 Expectations for Old Regular Baptist Ministers 79
14 I.D. Becomes a Preacher 85
15 The Establishment of Mt. Olivet O.R.B. Church ... 88
16 Trying to Support a Growing Family 94
17 Fatherhood 96
18 Vietnam 110
19 Politics 113
20 Doing "Church Work" 119
21 More of the Back Wit 127
22 Being a Grandfather 132
23 John Preece 134
24 Preaching and Singing 142
25 Offering Comfort and Fulfilling Duties in
    Uncomfortable Situations 148
26 A Preacher's Wife 155
27 Life After Ina Rose 161
28 I.D.'s Death 163
29 The Journal Entries 165
30 Home At Last 208
Bibliography 211

CHAPTER 1
The Town of Blackey

The Blackey Bridge
(Author's personal collection)

Blackey (pronounced BLACK-ee) is a small town nestled deep in the breathtakingly beautiful mountains of Southeastern Kentucky (specifically, the Cumberland Mountains) on the North Fork of the Kentucky River. Located in the county of Letcher, it is approximately sixteen miles from the county seat of Whitesburg.

Blackey is referred to as a city. Its citizens elect a mayor periodically, and they are served by a city council. The city has a water plant that provides city water for individuals who live either within the city limits of Blackey and/or along areas of Highway Seven. Until the plant was built a few years ago, locals had no access to city water and, thus, had to drill wells to allow water to be supplied to their homes.

Several churches are located in Blackey. It also gives residence to a small library, a senior citizens' center, Mountain Heritage Head Start, a small park, and Myrt's ATV Shop (owned by Ronnie and Myrtle Miller). The railroad runs through Blackey, and the occasional roar of a train whistle sounds as the trains that carry coal make their daily trips through that area.

There is a big, steel bridge that is painted a bright shade of blue, which connects the city of Blackey to Highway Seven. If one crosses this bridge to Highway Seven (or, as locals refer to it, Route Seven), C.B. Caudill's General Store immediately comes into view. An old, metal building still standing today, this store kept necessities such as sugar and flour in stock for many years. As recently as a few years ago, locals still gathered on the porch of that store to engage in relaxing conversation with then-owners Joe and Gaynell Caudill Begley (daughter of the now-deceased C.B. Caudill). Indeed, this store served members of the Blackey community for many years. Later, it was converted into a mini-museum of sorts. Today, it is not open for business; however, the building still remains a landmark in the area.

Blackey does have at least one significant claim to fame. It was in this area that scenes from the 1979 movie "Coal Miner's Daughter" (story of country singer Loretta Lynn's life) were filmed. I was a child at the time, but I still recall that the area was abuzz with excitement. Locals were trying to get roles in the film and catch a glimpse of film stars who were there for the filming. By the time my parents got me there, all of the children's roles had been filled. Hence, my big break into the world of show business was not to be. I did, however, get the opportunity to meet actress Sissy Spacek (who portrayed Loretta Lynn in the movie), and I was able to acquire her autograph. Several local people, including Ronnie and Sherry Back, did have small roles in the movie.

Blackey is not, by any means, a large city, though. In reality, it could be more accurately described as a small village filled with industrious residents who work hard to bring new businesses and updates into their community so that it will be a better place in which to dwell. Blackey is an area that is warm and inviting, and, on a summer afternoon, a passerby might see a few members of the community taking their daily walks around the circle encompassing the two railroad crossings. He might also see some local residents seated in rocking chairs on their porches and gently rocking to and fro, as they enjoy a gentle breeze on a warm day and observe the walkers who tred past their houses. A friendly "hello" (or "howdy," as locals might say) will likely be exchanged between walkers and porch-resters, for Blackey is a friendly community, where virtually everyone knows everyone else and outsiders are immediately recognized as "ferners" (foreigners).

There was a time in past years, however, when the quaint description provided above did not apply to Blackey, Kentucky. Elderly residents who still reside in and near the area can recall a time when Blackey could best be described as a booming town.

On the hill, next to the Doermann Memorial Presbyterian Church, set a hospital that was served by Doctor Ison, and, later, by Dr. Lundy Adams. On Main Street, in the present location of the Mount Olivet Old Regular Baptist Church, community members gathered to view the latest flicks of the day, as a movie theater stood there at that time.

Just down the street from the theater was a hangout known as "Goebel Stamp's Place."

In the middle of the town sat the source of much of Blackey's excitement - the train depot. Here, citizens of Blackey were able to congregate and meet people from various areas (both within and outside of the county), for the train was a popular means of travel at that time. Not only did it carry Blackey citizens to other areas, but it also carried visitors into the Blackey area.

On the right side of the hill, out from the hospital and the Presbyterian Church, there stood a school building. A long set of steps led from the bottom of the hill up to the area on which the school building was located.

This latter description of a booming town was more appropriate for the Blackey that existed in 1925, the year that I.D. Woodrow Back was born into the home of Callie and James "Little Jim" Back.

CHAPTER 2
Genealogy

In order to portray a truly accurate picture of exactly who I.D. Back was, this author feels that it important for her to take a brief moment to summarize his genealogy. Much of the information in this chapter was obtained from a resource entitled *A Back Family History: The Story of a Major Branch of the Back/Bach Family (Volumes 1 and 2)*. For a more elaborate search into the Back genealogy, the reader should refer to those texts.

The Backs of Blackey are descendants of a group of people, known as "Bachs," who emigrated from Germany. In fact, some descendants claim that one of the ancestors on a branch of their family tree was the famous musician Johan Sebastian Bach.

In Volume 1 of A *Back Family History: The Story of a Major Branch of the Back/Bach Family*, it was stated that Erich Bach (born somewhere between 1540 and 1550 in/near Freudenberg, Germany) "is the oldest known ancestor of our Bach/Back families of Kentucky, Virginia, and many other states." Per information recorded in that book, Erich Bach "was an official servant of an Earldom,"and he served as mayor and chief justice of Freudenberg for over 25 years. The authors of this book further state that Erich fathered two sons. One son was named Johan, and the other son was named Henrich. Henrich was the son through whom I.D. Back would one day descend.

The book referred to above also states that Henrich had a descendant named Hermann, and Hermann would be a "direct line ancestor of" I.D. Back. Per report of the authors, "In 1738, Hermann Bach and his wife...with their baby daughter Anna Ella, joined a group of men, women, and children who were authorized to emigrate from the Siegan area to the new English Colony of

Georgia, in North America." Hermann and his family actually ended up in Virginia. At some point, the authors report that "colonial officials recorded his name as Harman Back, a more Anglicized version of the German name Hermann Bach." The author's further report that, based on research conducted by Dr. Benjamin C. Holzclaw, "the first official mention he found of Harman Back was in what is now Culpepper County, Virginia."

After his move, Harman fathered four sons. According to the authors of the Back genealogy book, "two of his sons and several of his grandsons migrated to Kentucky after the Revolutionary War ended."

Harman's sons were named as follows: John, Joseph, Henry, and Harmon, Jr. Third son Henry was the father of several children, one of which was named John Back.

From John Back descended Henry J. Back. Henry J. Back fathered several children. One of these children was James G. Back. (Descendent Ronnie Back says that it is uncertain which name the "G" was meant to symbolize.)

James G. "Little Jim" Back was born on December 29, 1871. When he reached manhood, he initially married Julia Dixon. Julia, however, died on July 11, 1920. James G. Back's second marriage was to Callie Caudill Whitaker. (Callie, born February 5, 1889, was the daughter of William J. "Miller Bill" Caudill and his wife, Martha Whitaker Caudill. Callie was the granddaughter of "Stiller Bill" Caudill.) It was the union of James G. Back and Callie Caudill Whitaker that would produce I.D. Woodrow Back.

CHAPTER 3
Blackey's Newest Citizen

The date of I.D. Woodrow Back's birth was July 4, 1925. It was Independence Day, no less. This was a rather appropriate date for his birth, as the newest member of the Back family would grow to become a very patriotic man.

This July day in 1925 was likely hot and sweltering, as July days in Southeastern Kentucky so typically are. Also typical of July days in Kentucky is a humidity level that can be stifling at times. Thus, one can only imagine that weather conditions were uncomfortable during the time that young Callie Back lay in labor in the small, boxed house that rested upon a bank by the winding "River Road" in Blackey. (For those unfamiliar with the meaning of "boxed house," this simply refers to a house built in a particular fashion. Sleepers were placed horizontally, and the floor was nailed to them. Then, flat boards were nailed around the edges, and, finally, a roof was placed atop the house. The finished product contained walls that were approximately as thick as the boards. This was considered to be a very simple way to build a house, and, from what this author has learned, boxed houses were relatively common during the time that I.D. Back was a youngster.)

The yard at the Backs' house would have been cleanly swept, for, per I.D.'s own report, his mother never let a day pass without sweeping the yard. A stocky woman with hair swept atop her head in a bun, Callie has been described as "a strong person" by family and community members who knew her. As strong as she undoubtedly was, however, it still must have been a welcome relief when she heard the cry of her newborn babe and knew that her long hours of suffering through labor in that sweltering July heat had finally come to an end.

I.D. was to be the last child to which Callie gave birth. He was not, however, her first child. Married once before (at the age of fourteen) to Bill Whitaker (a tall, thin man with a small mustache), Callie came into the marriage to Jim Back with several children of her own in tow (Nancy "Skoffield," William "Bill" Whitaker II, Keller, Corsia, Ruth, and Vina).

As was stated in a previous chapter, Jim Back had also been married previously. So, he also brought a brood of his own (Madge, Bruce, James, and Gladys) into the union.

Elder J.T. Whitaker had married Callie and Jim on August 18, 1921. On that day, they began their married life together, along with Madge Back (age 14), Bruce Back (age 12), Glayds Back (age 9), James Back (age 4), Vina Whitaker (age 16), Ruth Whitaker (age 13), Keller Whitaker (age 10), Corsia Whitaker (age 8), Skoffield Whitaker (age 6), and William Whitaker II (age 4).

In 1922, on July 6, Callie had given birth to her first Back child. His name was to be John Paul. How the Back couple must have delighted in this new edition to their already-large brood! Unfortunately, John Paul was not to enjoy a long life. On August 18, 1928, he died, at the age of six-years-old, of causes unknown to this author. (This was not the first time that Callie had suffered the loss of a child. She had born several stillborn children during the time that she was married to Bill Whitaker. Also, she lost a young daughter named Susie to death, when the child was only five-years-old. Cause of Susie's death was unknown by those interviewed about this matter.)

On December 7, 1923, approximately two years and four months after their marriage, Jim and Callie added Walton Henry "Walt" Back to their family. Walton was to be the only "full" brother that I.D. would have, as he grew from childhood into manhood, but I.D.'s children insist that neither he nor Walt ever liked referring to their other siblings as "half" siblings. Instead, they both took the attitude that they were all brothers and sisters, and that there were no halves nor wholes to be considered.

In preparation for the writing of this book, the author was privileged to interview I.D.'s older brother, Keller Whitaker, who has since died. During this interview, Keller would recall that the Back family and Whitaker family meshed uncommonly well. Just as I.D. and Walt had resisted the notion of referring to "half" and "whole" siblings, Keller remembered that neither the Back children nor the Whitaker children referred to each other as stepbrothers and stepsisters. He remembered that, upon the day that Jim Back (who Keller described as being a kind man for whom the Whitaker children immediately began to feel love) and Callie Whitaker united in marriage, all children involved considered themselves to be members of one, big family - not two separate families.

Still, it is true that a special bond did develop between young I.D. Back and his older brother Walton. This is likely due not so much to the fact that they were "whole brothers," but to the fact that they were the two youngest children in the family. They were closer in age to each other than to any of their other siblings. At any rate, they had a special relationship and were, according to Ronnie Back, "as close as two brothers could be."

Despite their close relationship, however, Keller recalled that I.D. and Walt were quite different in nature. He remembered Walt as being the quieter and more studious of the two. Walt was an individual who applied himself to completing a given task. In contrast, what I.D. wanted most in the world was to just enjoy life and have a good time.

CHAPTER 4
School Days

From that 1925 Independence Day when I.D. first entered the world, until the time of his death, he was physically small in stature. Per reports of those close to the family, this was a trait inherited from the Backs, who tended toward small stature. In contrast, I.D.'s Whitaker siblings have been described as being slightly larger than average. At his greatest height, I.D. was approximately 5'8" tall. By the time of his death, age and osteoporosis had shrunken him to a mere 5'6". As the old adage proclaims, however, "Dynamite comes in small packages."

And dynamite he was! Keller Whitaker recalled that he was "full of life" as a youngster. He also recalled that the mischievous little boy was, as the baby of the family, "petted" by both of his parents. He could often avoid punishment simply by rolling his eyes up sweetly at his mother. If this didn't work, he was very adept at talking his mother out of spanking him. According to Keller, I.D.'s skills in persuasion were such that "he would have made a good lawyer."

Keller laughingly recalled one instance, however, in which young I.D., despite his attempts to influence his mother through sweet expressions and convincing words, was unable to dissuade Callie from punishing him. [Lest the reader think that I.D. was physically abused as a child, the author wishes to preface this story with a reminder that, at the time that I.D. was growing up, children were punished differently than they are today. At that time, spankings or "whippings"(as residents of Southeastern Kentucky might call them) were delivered via hand or "switches" (small tree limbs) as a common form of discipline. Time-outs, etc. would not become popular until later years. These spankings were administered strictly as a means of punishment for disobedience or some other form of childhood transgression. They were not administered simply to hurt the child, but as a means of discipline. There is a difference between discipline and abuse, and the reader must keep in mind that I.D. received spankings as a means of discipline. That being said, the author hopes and trusts that the reader will see humor in this particular anecdote.]

I.D. had misbehaved one day. Although his brother could no longer remember what trespass he had committed, it had been severe enough to meet with his mother's disapproval. A limb cut from a nearby peach tree was the tool that Callie was going to use to ensure that I.D. was punished for this particular instance of misbehavior.

According to those who knew him, I.D. was always a very hyperkinetic child. Thus, he was exhibiting typical behavior, as he tried to avoid his mother by skipping around the yard in short pants commonly worn by young boys in that time. As he attempted to skip outside his mother's reach, she ran behind him, striving to swat his short legs with her switch.

Keller recalled I.D. crying out, in that dramatic manner so often used by children, that his mother was killing him! As proof of the torture that she had inflicted upon him, he admonished her to just look at the blood running down his legs! By this time, his spanking was finished and, with a twinkle of amusement in her eye, Callie promptly told I.D., "No, Son. Blood is red." He had urinated on himself, and urine, not blood, was the liquid that he had felt on his legs!

Lest there had been doubt before about young I.D.'s tendency toward mischief, an incident occurring on his first day of school ("primer," as he referred to it) would remove any of that doubt.

One can only imagine the excitement and anxiety that the small boy with the wide forehead, dancing blue eyes, and short, blond hair felt as he walked hand-in-hand with his mother to his first day of class at the Blackey Public School.

A four-room brick building, the schoolhouse, as was mentioned previously, sat atop a hill between the Presbyterian Church and what is now the Blackey Missionary Baptist Church. (The school building reportedly burned at some point during the 1970's.) Though small in comparison to today's schools, the schoolhouse must have seemed daunting to the little boy who, prior to this day, had spent very little time away from his mother. (In fact, during an interview conducted in later years, he would still use the word "big" when describing the building.) He surely must have clung tightly to his mother's hand, as they entered this new world together.

As the day progressed and little I.D. became better acquainted with his new surroundings and his new teacher, Miss Susie, however, he became more relaxed. He actually began enjoying this new adventure as a primer student. By the time the children were dismissed for recess, in fact, he had become so comfortable that he dared to venture away from his teacher and his fellow students so that he might succumb to temptations provided by one of the creeks that ran along each side of the school.

As recess ended and the other children began congregating around the teacher in preparation to go back inside the building, Miss Susie noticed that young I.D. was not among her brood. How frantic the young teacher must have been when she realized that one of her students was missing! The brief moments that she spent looking for her young charge must have seemed like hours. Finally, however, she did locate him...wading in the creek! That is how it came to be that little I.D. Back received a paddling on his very first day of school.

Via interviews with people who can remember those days, this author has learned that the relationship between parents and teachers was somewhat different at that time than it is in today's world. Today, corporal punishment has been banned from school systems. If a child is punished in any way, some parents will automatically side with the child against the teacher. Lawsuits are even filed against teachers at times. In those days, however, a child who received a spanking in school could expect no sympathy at home. What he could expect is to get a second spanking at home as punishment for the first one that he got at school.

My grandfather, D.Y. Fields, who was a year younger than I.D., used to tell me a story that gave evidence to this information. He said that his teacher spanked him at school one day. That afternoon, he made the mistake of telling his mother Eliza about the incident, in hopes that she might sympathize with him. He said that his mother responded by saying, "Oh, Honey. Pull your little breeches down and let Mommy see what that ole teacher did to you." When he lowered his pants, she swatted him again!

Although, as has been mentioned, Callie could sometimes be influenced by I.D.'s sweet expressions and influential arguments against punishment, she was, at heart, a strict disciplinarian. Hence, it was unlikely that she would be an exception to the rule that parents spanked children who were spanked at school. When I.D. came home from school that evening and tearfully told his mother that he had received a "whipping" on his very first day of primer, Callie did nothing but bend him over and swat his little buttocks again!

Throughout his elementary school years, I.D. continued attending classes at the Blackey Public School. While the spanking acquired on his first day of primer was the first discipline measure to be inflicted upon him at the old schoolhouse, it was definitely not to be the last one. Several years older than his baby brother, Keller Whitaker was hired as a principal at the school during the time that I.D. was in attendance there. Keller would recall years later that, during that time, I.D. once got in trouble for hugging a pretty little girl in class. He was brought before Mr. Whitaker so that he might be disciplined for his actions. At that point, young I.D. was questioned as to why he would do such a thing as hug this little girl, when he was well aware that such actions were not allowed at this school house. "Oh," he replied, "I don't know. I guess I just took a huggin' spell!"

During the latter years of his elementary school career, I.D. was hired by a teacher named Dana Ison to, during the winter months, carry in firewood and keep a fire built in the old potbelly stove that warmed their school. His wages for a week's work were to be 85 cents. When I.D. recounted this story during his interview with this author, I attempted to verify his salary by inquiring, "Per week?"

"Yes!" he responded, with a twinkle in his eye. Then, in demonstration of that quick wit for which he was so well known in the community, he added, "Cash!"

It must have seemed to those in the community, his home, and his school that young I.D. was forever engaged in some sort of mischievous act. In fact, his earliest practice in the area of "preaching" came during his childhood years. I.D.'s mother was a devout Christian who regularly attended services at the Old Regular Baptist churches in the area. Hence, young I.D. was very familiar, as were many of his young peers whose parents also attended these church services, with the nature of the Old Regular Baptist ministers' method of delivering sermons.

Those individuals familiar with the Old Regular Baptist ministry understand that these ministers are not usually schooled at seminaries. They become ministers because they feel that God has "called" them to do so. (There will be more in-depth discussion about this topic in a subsequent chapter.) Thus, while many of the ministers are well-read and knowledgeable in regard to Biblical verses and lessons, they do not often have the soft, practiced delivery method of a more-reserved minister from some of the other church denominations in the world. This is not being revealed to the reader as a form of criticism, for this author has attended Old Regular Baptist church services for years and has the utmost respect for the Old Regular Baptist preachers. I have also attended enough services in other churches, however, to know that, if someone is used to hearing a preacher from another denomination and is not familiar with the delivery method used by Old Regular Baptist preachers, then that visitor is going to be surprised during his or her first visit to an Old Regular Baptist church!

The preachers generally use relatively soft voices and just talk to the crowd a bit when they first stand to deliver their sermons. A minister might say something such as, "I'm glad and thankful that the Lord has blessed me to be in your presence another day." If he is blessed to truly preach that day, it will be because the Spirit of the Lord has come upon him. As this happens and the sermon progresses, his volume increases. Sentences often become separated by a long inhalation of breath that sounds as if he's saying, "Uh!" or "Ah!"in a staccato fashion. The minister rarely stands in one place during the entire sermon. His hand is frequently raised to the side of his head, as he walks around the pulpit (and sometimes down the aisle of the church or out into the congregation) preaching the Gospel. Occasionally, a preacher will become so overwhelmed by the wondrous feeling that accompanies God's Spirit that, as the sermon progresses, he will jump for joy and raise both hands in the air.

Songs in the Old Regular Baptist churches are also sung in a manner that is different from that of songs sung by congregations in other denominations. There is no choir. Hymn books are not provided to every member of the congregation. There is no instrumental accompaniment. Instead, a lone male singer (who does hold a hymn book) begins a song by singing its initial line (or a portion of the initial line) solo. When he finishes singing this line, he calls out, in a lilting voice, the next line of the song. At that point, the congregation as a whole sings in unison the line that the song leader just announced. This practice is called "lining," and, at the Smithsonian Institute in Washington, D.C., there are tapes on which this practice is demonstrated.

So, as the reader can deduce, the characteristics of the delivery of sermons and songs in the Old Regular Baptist Churches are quite a bit different from those exhibited among other church denominations. Because of this, young I.D. and some of the other children in the area found it humorous to mimic the preachers and singers. They enjoyed "playing church."

I.D. Back was never a perfect man, and he would not want anyone to say otherwise. In time, he became a good, Christian man, who strove to live his life in a manner that was pleasing unto God. Still, even then, he was not perfect. If he was not perfect as a Christian, then he was certainly not perfect in the days preceding his salvation. He did make mistakes in life.

One of the mistakes that he made was mimicking these preachers called by God to preach His Word. This is a very dangerous thing to do, as the preachers and members of the Old Regular Baptist churches are generally good, Christian people who are trying their best to serve God in the manner that they feel is pleasing to Him. Thus, to mock or make fun of Christian people and holy ways leaves one's soul in danger of eternal damnation, and I.D. Back would have been one of the first people, after he became a Christian, to discourage others from engaging in such antics. He would not have wanted the reader to infer that, because he made the mistake of "playing church," it is acceptable to do these things.

This author believes that God often winks at the mistakes of children who do things in ignorance. If I.D. had reached the age of accountability by the time that he behaved in this manner, then he repented of these actions later. At any rate, God had mercy on him and forgave him. Thus, I hope that neither God nor the reader will be offended in any way by the stories that are about to be recounted.

Young I.D., during the early years of his life, had seen so many preachers deliver fiery sermons from the pulpit that he had become quite adept at mimicking both their actions and the cadence of their voices. Thus, when a cat or dog died in the community, it was not unusual for this young boy and his friends to hold a "funeral service" for the deceased animal. They would lay the animal's corpse out for public viewing, and then a group of children would congregate for the funeral. I.D. would often begin the "service" by lining a song. Then, he would begin "preaching."Undoubtedly, he jumped up and down and yelled out instructions from the Bible (as well as instructions that he had invented on his own), as his mischievous peers goaded him on with shouts of "Amen" and "Preach it, Brother."

There is one story related to this issue that was recounted to this author by I.D.'s daughter, Sherry Fugate. She stated that an elderly resident of Blackey was supposedly sitting on his porch during one of the children's "church services." Upon hearing I.D.'s "sermon," the old man reportedly said something along the lines of "Who is that wonderful preacher?" The elderly gentleman had heard the chants and cadences that young I.D. so skillfully mimicked, and he mistakenly thought that the mischievous lad was a real preacher preaching a real sermon.

My own father relayed a similar story to me. He said that, on one occasion, a resident of Blackey heard young I.D. "preaching" during one of the "funeral services." Upon learning that the person he was hearing was the mischievous lad who was so prone to misbehave, the resident said, "Hmph! If I didn't know better, I'd say he was called to preach!"

Upon completing elementary school, I.D. entered high school at Stuart Robinson School. Located approximately one mile north of the Blackey Bridge, this campus is still in existence, and it is breathtakingly beautiful. Sprawling green lawns shaded by towering trees continue to give home to a softball field and ancient brick buildings that were standing at the time that I.D. attended school there. A few, newer buildings also dot the campus today and serve as locales for class reunions, Christmas parties, etc.

Stuart Robinson has not been a public school since Letcher Elementary and High School were opened. It did serve as a private, Christian school for a while, but that is no longer the case. In the years falling between its time as a public school and its time as a private school for children in elementary and secondary grade levels, it still served as a place of education for many of the area's college students. During those years, it was referred to as Calvary College.

During his years at Stuart Robinson High School, I.D. made many friends. Two of his closest friends, however, were boys that he'd known long before he began attending school at Stuart Robinson. Their names were Van Dixon and Wakefield Back. Wakefield was actually I.D.'s nephew. While Wakefield and I.D. were in the same class, Van was a school year ahead of his two buddies. When asked if the threesome ever got into troublesome situations in school, I.D. refused to reveal any juicy details. He simply said that they got along well, and he remembered that they never got into any serious trouble.

Wakefield is deceased now. He died as the result of an injury incurred during the war. Van's current residence was unknown to the author at the time of this book's publication. Thus, neither of these two men could be interviewed to determine what types of antics the threesome might have been involved in during their high school years. Given I.D.'s mischievous nature, however, it is difficult for this author to fathom the notion that the boys did not encounter at least some mischief during their days at Stuart Robinson High School.

Always a sports fan, I.D. became a member of the basketball team during his high school years. (He had used a self-made, cloth ball when learning to play the game.) He played the position of forward. Due to his small stature, he was referred to in later years by his son Tony as "a two-foot forward." In modesty, I.D. proclaimed to this author that he really was "not much of a ball player in those days." Upon hearing his father make this modest claim, Tony exclaimed, "Did he say he wasn't any good?! Don't let him fool you. He was good. He has a golden basketball to prove it!"

CHAPTER 5
Life at Home

I.D. Back was blessed with much happiness during his childhood days. He was surrounded by brothers and sisters who doted upon him. Siblings who were close to his age, as well as the children belonging to some of his older siblings, ensured that he was never at a loss for playmates.

Growing up during the years of the Great Depression, he, like many other children of that time, lacked many of the materialistic treasures that children of today possess. Instead of purchasing toys at some retail store, I.D. and his siblings had to craft their toys by hand. For example, he would fashion a ball by "wadding" a piece of cloth into a spherical form if he wanted to engage his friends and family in a friendly game of baseball. "Round Town," a game similar to baseball, was popular among I.D. and his peers.

While lacking material goods, however, there was lack of neither love nor laughter in the Back household. Even everyday events associated with household chores could be transformed into humorous stories. One such story centers around the time that Callie sent Jim Back to buy a workhorse that would be able to assist with the plowing. All of the children still living at home, but particularly I.D. and Walton, were so excited at the prospect of seeing this new horse that they could hardly wait for their father to return home with his new acquisition.

Soon, the children saw Jim Back nearing home. As the man and his horse drew nearer, however, the young boys noticed that the animal walked in a rather strange manner. Before progressing forward, it would carefully step one foot outward in front, and then the other foot would follow. The boys laughed, as they commented that the horse looked as if it was trying to feel, rather than see, where it was going. As it turned out, that is exactly what the horse was doing. Just as Jim neared the yard, Callie came out of the house and saw her husband and his new horse. "Lord have mercy, Jim Back!" she exclaimed. "You've gone out and bought an old, blind horse!" Jim had not realized, when he was purchasing the horse, that it suffered from blindness.

Despite all of the happy experiences occurring in I.D.'s youth, however, these years were not without sad moments and turmoil, as well. One of the saddest events in his young life occurred in 1941. One evening in June, Jim Back returned home as usual from a long day at work. He was not acting in his usual manner on this day, however. Reportedly, he walked slowly to the porch and then stopped at the bottom of the porch steps and said, "Callie, you're gonna have to help pull me in this evening." Shortly after she helped him inside, he suffered a stroke. Within a few days, on June 8, 1941, I.D.'s beloved father passed from this world into eternal life.

Jim's death left his widowed wife in a difficult position. While most of her children had already reached adulthood and moved out of her home to start their own families, she still had some children (including grandson Wakefield Back, whom she helped raise) living under her roof. She was left to provide for these children the same services that she had always provided as a mother (e.g., cooking dinner, washing clothes). Now, however, she would also have the responsibility of seeing that those chores previously performed by her husband were also completed.

Callie would not be defeated by her husband's death, however. She was human, and, undoubtedly, her heart was broken when her husband died. She realized, though, that no matter how heartbroken she was, the old adage that "life goes on" is definitely true. She had a household to run. She had chores to complete. She had children to feed, and, at that time, there were no welfare checks that she could rely upon for assistance. Individuals in need had to grow their own food or face starvation. Callie was not about to let her family starve. So, after a short period of mourning, she wiped her tears, on the day of her husband's death, and, as she had done everyday in the past for so many years now, she headed outside to milk the cow and perform her other daily chores. This behavior was reportedly seen in Callie time after time, when members of her family died. No matter how sad she felt, she knew that chores had to be done, and so she did them.

Some of the chores that she performed after her husband's death involved relatively hard labor. She would not be deterred, however. Family friend Elwood Cornett remembers seeing her empty out her barn each year and spread manure on her garden with the help of a horse and sled. He also recalls seeing her plow the garden.

Per I.D.'s own words in later years, his mother was "a rock that held the family together when Daddy died." She maintained her strength in these troubling years and held her family together primarily through prayer, her faith in God, and her willingness to work for those things that she and her family needed for survival.

Callie's belief in hard work was not only applicable to herself. She also believed that her children should work. Thus, she sometimes enlisted the help of I.D. and Walton. Among the tasks that she sometimes assigned to I.D. was the job of hoeing the garden, while Walton plowed.

Those familiar with proper gardening procedures used in those days know that, when hoeing corn, the plowing was to be done first. That would mean that, after Walton plowed, I.D. was to come behind him and hoe the corn. Apparently, however, I.D. had not been schooled in proper gardening procedures.

Family friend Beulah Back recalled the story with amusement. Apparently, Callie had sent I.D. and Walton into the garden one day. A few hours after sending them outside to work, Callie saw I.D. coming back into the house alone. Walton was not with him. Curious about the matter, Callie inquired as to whether or not the two boys had completed their chores. To this question, I.D. responded, "I've finished hoeing, but Walt still has a little more plowing to do." He had hoed in front of, rather than behind, Walton!

In later years, I.D. would continue to show little interest in the art of gardening. Ronnie Back remembers that I.D.'s natural "green thumb" frustrated Walt. Walt would take classes on horticulture/gardening, etc. during his years in the army. However, when it came to raising produce, I.D., despite his reported lack of care for the state of his garden, had more success than Walt did.

This frustration was evident during a conversation that Walton had in later years. Reportedly, Walt was speaking one evening with an elderly female member of the community. Walt was still a sinner, and, by the time that this conversation occurred, I.D. had received salvation. Per a friend's recollection, the old lady said to Walt, "Walton, Honey, why don't you try to straighten up and be more like your little brother?" Like I.D., Walt possessed a quick wit. When he heard the lady's question, he turned to her and said, "In what way? Plant a garden and then let the weeds take it over?"

Aside from prayer, faith, and hard work, Callie had another secret for keeping her household intact during these difficult years. She continued her practice of disciplining her children as necessary, despite the fact that they were nearing adulthood.

One New Year's Eve, at Mt. Olivet Old Regular Baptist Church's annual watch night service, I.D. shared with the congregation one particular incident in which his mother had disciplined him. (For those unfamiliar with the term "watch night service," this refers to a December 31st church gathering at which those in attendance eat, fellowship, sing hymns, and reminisce about the blessings that God has bestowed upon them in the year that's about to end. They strive to be on their knees in prayer at the moment that the old year ends and the New Year begins. During these watch night services, several of the preachers stand and say a few words. Some just talk informally for a few minutes. Others actually preach.)

I clearly recall seeing I.D. standing near the pulpit that year. I do not recall everything he said, but I do know that, at some point, he veered off into a story from his boyhood. (I.D. frequently used incidents from everyday life to emphasize a Biblical teaching that he was trying to impart to members of the congregation.) During the telling of this particular story, he spoke of coming into his mother's kitchen one day and saying something that she interpreted as being "smart-alecky" (i.e., disrespectful). Upon hearing I.D.'s words of disrespect, Callie took the rag that she had been using to wash dishes and promptly "sworped" I.D. with it. When she did this, I.D. would later recall that the old, wet, greasy dishrag just wrapped around his head. (Again, the author wishes to remind the reader that children were dealt with in the 1930's and 1940's in a manner that is somewhat different than the way that today's children are dealt with. This was simply Callie's means of bringing quick discipline to a disrespectful child. She was not being abusive.)

When I.D. finished his story, an uproar of laughter arose from the congregation. Among the preachers seated behind him on the stand was my father. That is one reason that I recall this story so well. Dad is one of those people who, upon being amused, has great difficulty controlling his laughter. So, even after I.D.'s story was completed and the rest of the people inside the church had stopped laughing, Dad still sat there shaking with laughter. I.D., knowing that Dad had a laugh that would come easily but end only with great effort, just turned around and looked at him with a twinkle in his eye.

During his teenage years, however, I.D. was faced with issues much more important than dodging dish rags. At this point in his life, trouble was brewing on a worldwide level. An evil dictator named Adolph Hitler was rapidly gaining power, not only in his own country of Germany, but also (as he was planning to invade other areas of the world) worldwide. As history tells us, the United States had tried to avoid involvement in this conflict. Then, on December 7, 1941, an event happened that would change our country's stance regarding involvement. The Japanese bombed a United States military base in Pearl Harbor, Hawaii.

This event put the young Back men in a difficult position. I.D. had not yet completed his education. He was only a sophomore in high school.

Keller Whitaker would later recall that the large age gap between Callie's older Whitaker children, and the older Back children, and I.D. and Walt Back resulted in I.D. and Walt having a host of adult siblings nearby, who could act as counselors and sources of advice. Keller would recall offering the two boys advice about various matters in the absence of their now-deceased father. Undoubtedly, the two were flooded with advice regarding whether or not to fight in the war, and Callie was reportedly frantic with worry.

In today's world, there continues to be wars and rumors of wars (as predicted in the Holy Bible). However, it would be virtually unthinkable for members of today's society to fathom the idea of asking a high school student to drop out of school and travel miles across the ocean to fight against foreign soldiers. It would be particularly unthinkable for us to ask a young man or woman who had just lost one parent, and knew that he or she was badly needed at home by the other parent, to make such a sacrifice.

In the first days of 1942, however, that was just the predicament that young I.D. and Walton Back were facing. Both boys knew that they were needed at home to help Callie. If they enlisted for military service at this point, she would be alone and left to do all the daily chores without help. They also knew, however, that their country needed soldiers to help fight the enemy and preserve the freedom of their fellow Americans. In the end, I.D. and Walt, always patriotic, decided that their country needed them more than their mother did at the time. They would volunteer to become American soldiers.

CHAPTER 6
Military Service

Walton Back, along with next-door neighbor Van Dixon (who, as the reader will recall, had also been one of I.D.'s closest high school chums), enlisted for military service. Walt had planned to enlist in the cavalry. Always a horse lover, he felt that this was the branch of service that would be most enjoyable to him. Soon after Walt's enlistment, however, the cavalry was dismounted. Hence, he enlisted in the paratroopers.

In later years, I.D. would tell this author that he wanted the older boys to know that he could do just as much as they could ("was just as big as they were"). He didn't like the idea of his brother and friend going to war without him. So, he quit school and enlisted in the United States army on November 6, 1942. Walton forged their mother's signature so that the underage I.D. would be permitted to enlist.

Upon forging this signature, however, Walton admonished his younger brother that, despite his own enlistment in the paratroopers, this is not the group that he wanted I.D. to join. The protective older brother felt that this particular branch of service would provide too much risk to young I.D.'s life. He promptly informed I.D. that he would "whip" him if he so much as thought about enlisting in the paratroopers. So, I.D. would enlist in the infantry.

His place of enlistment was Fort Benjamin Harrison, Indiana. There were some minor complications upon his attempt to enter military service. For one thing, the name printed on his birth certificate read as "I.D. Woodrow Back." There is some indication that his mother meant for the initials I.D. to be given in honor of the names "Isaac" and "Dixon." Both of these names were relatively common at the time of I.D.'s birth.

Furthermore, I.D. had an uncle named Isaac Dixon Caudill, and there is some speculation that he may have been named after this uncle. Apparently, however, Callie never shared this information with I.D., nor did she have any such information recorded on his birth certificate. Upon trying to register for army enlistment, he learned that the army would not accept initials as names. Those individuals in charge of the enlistment process wanted to know exactly what those initials stood for. So, per report of Beulah Back, who had heard I.D.'s brother Keller tell the story in later years, I.D. had written home and said, "Ma, What's my name?"

Another obstacle to enlistment came in the form of an Army general. During the registration process, this general likely recognized that young I.D. was not nearly as old as he might have wanted others to believe. Upon meeting I.D., the short, plump, balding, bespectacled general inquired, "Soldier, are you sure that you want to join the army?" Upon hearing I.D.'s affirmative response, the general added, "Well, just remember, before making up your mind about that, that I was six-feet, four-inches tall and had the prettiest head of hair you've ever seen before I joined the infantry!" I.D. was not deterred. His registration was approved, and he was now enlisted in the United States Army.

Initially, I.D. was stationed at Camp Butler, North Carolina. He served there for 18 months, before transferring to Camp Blanded, Florida. After Camp Blanded, he served at Camp Picket, Virginia. Next, he traveled to Camp Kilner, New Jersey. After Camp Kilner, he was sent overseas.

He was going to be stationed in Germany. His beloved Walton had already been sent overseas in May 1944. The two had been allowed to remain together for a short time before basic training began. Afterwards, however, they had been separated. Now, four months after Walt had been sent to fight in the Pacific, it was September 1944, and I.D.'s journey was about to begin.

In later years, he would recall boarding a ship in New York. There were approximately 1500 other soldiers who were boarding the ship with him. During the trip to Germany, he sailed to Barmouth, England, went across the English Channel with a troop, went through the Seine River, and traveled across France in the back of a truck. As he was riding in back of the truck, he was looking into the sky. Suddenly, he saw a buzz bomb exploding overhead.

What an adventure this must have been for this young teen, who had never before traveled beyond the hills of Southeastern Kentucky. Ronnie would recall I.D. saying in later years that the war was the only thing that ever took him out of Blackey!

According to Ronnie, it was also during the trip to Germany that I.D. first became acquainted with Bernie Reed. Their initial meeting took place in Chase City, Virginia, where the two encountered some trouble when they accidentally broke a window. During this meeting, however, the pair could not know that one would eventually end up saving the life of the other in a battle yet to come.

It seemed that I.D.'s knack for getting into troublesome situations had followed him into military service. Aside from this incident with the broken window, there had been other mishaps. He had managed to break his arm during basic training in North Carolina. He had also managed, in the words of his son Ronnie, to "bang himself up" in a jeep wreck in Europe. Ronnie has laughingly stated that I.D. "was hurt two or three times before combat ever began!"

Unfortunately, his string of misfortunate accidents did not end when combat began. In fact, Ronnie recollects that I.D. was not involved in combat for a very long period of time before he was injured yet again.

I.D.'s specialty military occupation was field lineman. A field lineman's job is to carry and string wire, in addition to his regular duties as a foot soldier. Paired with I.D., as he carried out his duties as a field lineman, was his old buddy, Bernie Reed. The two worked as a team. One was required to carry guns, while the other strung wire.

On the day of I.D.'s injury, the Battle of the Bulge was in progress. (This author was never privileged to speak with Mr.Reed; hence, the account of details surrounding the time that I.D. and Bernie spent together is based upon what she learned from Ronnie Back.) I.D. and Bernie had been out together on what Bernie would later describe to Ronnie Back as "a bad patrol." While stringing wire, the two had been attacked by snipers. As the person designated to carry the guns on this day, I.D. was the one who had been forced to return fire against their attackers. After the shooting had stopped, I.D., uncertain as to whether or not any of his bullets had actually hit one of the snipers, was worried about the possibility that he might have just taken the life of another human being. Even if one does shoot in self-defense, the realization that one has killed another person would likely be a difficult concept for most people, especially people as young as I.D. was at this time, to accept. Having been raised by Christian parents, he knew that killing another person is a sin, and it's unlikely that he was, at that time, receiving much comfort from the thought that he had (possibly) killed someone in an act of self-defense during a time of war.

Ronnie recalls that his father would not speak of this patrol in later years. Bernie has told Ronnie in recent years, however, that he believed I.D. to be upset over this patrol. This is perhaps the reason that, when the two later entered the basement of an abandoned building in an attempt to escape the Germans' repeated shelling, I.D. simply retreated to a corner and lowered his head.

Seconds after I.D. lowered his head with worry, a shell blasted into the basement. The room exploded, and the impact of the explosion sent young I.D. flying across the room. He landed, unconscious, in the rubble of the destroyed building. In the midst of all this chaos, Bernie Reed threw himself across the body of his friend. Still, when the bombing had ended and the damages were being assessed, I.D. was laid out with the dead.

Bernie, however, who had dragged I.D. out of the building, came to his rescue yet again by exclaiming, "Hey! Back's still alive! He's not dead!" At that point, I.D. was recounted among the living. He was one of only three soldiers from that building to survive the explosion.

Although he was still alive, the young man from Blackey, Kentucky had been injured, and medical attention was needed. In order that he might receive this appropriate medical attention, I.D. was loaded onto a hospital train and sent to a hospital in Cherbourg, France. That was to be his place of residence during the remainder of his stay overseas.

While I.D. was recuperating in a military hospital, Bernie continued fighting in the war. The two would be reunited several decades later.

During I.D.'s stay in the military hospital, many significant events took place internationally. Adolph Hitler met his death. United States President Franklin D. Roosevelt, who I.D. would describe in later years as the best President ever to serve during his lifetime, died in office. Vice-President Harry Truman replaced him as Commander in Chief. It was also in this French military hospital that I.D. received the news that he had long been waiting to hear...the Germans had surrendered.

After Germany's surrender, patients were the first individuals to be shipped back home. Hence, I.D. would soon be on his way back to his beloved United States of America. He would later remember that, while he was resting on the boat, he kept looking in the distance for the Statue of Liberty. As they had sailed out of New York on his trip to Germany, he assumed that that would be the location at which the returning ship would dock. Instead, however, they docked in Boston, Massachusetts. From there, he sailed to Florida, where the soldiers were assigned to barracks. I.D. took up residence at Welch Convalescent Center in Daytona Beach.

Elder Ivan Amburgey, upon being interviewed by this author, recalled I.D. telling him that he had remained at this convalescent center in Florida (for rehabilitation purposes) for six months, before returning home to Kentucky. During his time at the convalescent center, I.D. was reportedly allowed to engage in relaxing activities such as walking the beach. He was also allowed time for meditation about the war in general, his role in that war, and the life in Kentucky that he would be returning to in the near future.

[I.D. would, years later, recount to Elder Amburgey the story of an incident, which happened during his time at the convalescent center, that would return to haunt him in the years following his own acquisition of salvation. He would remember being on the beach, drinking with a fellow army buddy. As the two sat drinking on the beach, an elderly gentleman (who, as they later learned, was a minister) approached them and began testifying to them about how and why they needed to "clean up" their lives. The two young soldiers ignored the words of wisdom that the old man was imparting to them. In fact, I.D.'s friend used profane language when he spoke to the gentleman. In the words of Elder Amburgey, the friend "cussed the man out."

Amburgey would recall I.D. telling him that, when he later thought about this situation (i.e., what that old man had tried to do for him and his comrade, and the way the two of them had acted in return), his heart broke. Even though he had not been the individual who did the cursing, I.D. professed that he felt guilty for sitting by and neglecting to rebuke his comrade.]

While he was ecstatic to be back in his beloved United States of America, and to know that his duty in the war had been served, I.D.'s happiness was diminished by the fact that the Japanese had not yet surrendered. Hence, Walton Back was still in the heat of battle. Uncertainty regarding Walt's safety brought the younger brother great concern.

Alas, however, the Americans dropped the atomic bombs on Japan, and the Japanese surrendered. I.D. would later recall being so happy to hear the news of the Japanese surrender and World War II's end that he jumped out of a window in Daytona Beach! He remembered that fellow soldiers laughed, pointed at him, and exclaimed, "Look! Back jumped out of a window!" Needless to say, he was not the only happy soldier. I.D. would also recall that a group of happy marines celebrated the war's end by driving a car into the ocean and then swimming back to the shore. All seemed well with the world again, for the war had finally ended.

On September 24, 1945, Walter T. Becker (Walter T. Becker, Lt. Col. MC, Executive Officer) signed a discharge for I.D. Back (15335236, Technician 5th grade, 810th signal service battalion). The dispersing officer was H.L. Reed. He was awarded with a good conduct medal and the European-African-Middle Eastern Service Medal. He did not receive a Purple Heart for the injuries that he received. Reason given was that no blood was shed.

Despite the lack of bloodshed, however, the injuries sustained during the Battle of the Bulge would affect him for the rest of his natural life. Until the day of his death, he would continue to suffer the repercussions of this accident. It's generally known that he recuperated from these injuries and went on to live a relatively long life. What is not so commonly known, however, is that the explosion had rendered him with a concussion from which he would never completely recover. There were times when he would have difficulty breathing. In fact, he sometimes had so much difficulty breathing that his face would suddenly turn very red. This was particularly the case if he became very upset over something. Also, as a result of his involvement in the war, I.D. exhibited characteristics of someone who is, as laymen say, "shell-shocked." These factors interacted to result in his being a very nervous person in years following his return from the war.

Because of the injuries that he sustained in the war, I.D. was rated as 100% disabled when he was released from the military. Hence, he would receive a disability pension for a time. However, the amount of the pension was not very significant.

His "mustering out pay" (money given to a soldier who was leaving the service) was $300. He received this money in 3 installments equaling $100 each. Ronnie, with a shake of his head and a twinkle in his eye, said that his father "had him a time on that." As he received that money when he was still a sinner, one can only imagine the amount of liquor that it must have been used to purchase!

In addition to "mustering out pay," he received travel pay equaling $48.90. With this money, he was able to pay for a bus ride home, through Abingdon, Virginia.

In later years, I.D. would recall exiting the train at the old, familiar train depot in Blackey. After getting off the train, he trekked along the familiar route of the "River Road," which would lead him to his home. As the old home place started coming into view, the first thing that he saw was a lady in a bonnet, plowing the garden via use of a mule. The bonnet-covered head looked up. The woman saw the young soldier coming toward her home. She began to run toward the soldier, and the soldier began to run toward her. When they met, she, with tear-filled eyes, embraced him in her arms. Alas, he had returned to the arms of his mother.

While shedding tears, Callie exclaimed, "Oh, my baby! Baby, let Mommy look at you and see what they've done to you!" I.D. would recall that Callie looked at him from head to toe so that she could be sure that he was not injured. It was a joyful day at the Back home.

CHAPTER 7
Working and Playing in Post-War Years

Upon returning to Letcher County, Kentucky, I.D. attempted to return to high school to complete the educational experience that the war had interrupted. He soon learned, however, that the effects that the war had had upon him were such that he would not be able to complete school now. By this point in his life, he simply had neither the patience nor the health needed to complete high school. So, he began looking for a job.

After returning from the war, he tried several different jobs. Although this author has questioned a variety of individuals about the matter, no one seems to be certain which job I.D. tried first. None of his jobs yielded a great amount of money. Nevertheless, they did provide him with more money than he would be able to get via his disability pension (which he lost when he began working). This was important to I.D., as he needed money with which to fund his sinful lifestyle.

Several of his jobs involved work in and around the coal mines (e.g., driving coal trucks). Hence, he now could afford to buy even more liquor than before! Old family friend, Ray Back, recalls that "it took the little 'fellar' quite a while to settle down" after he returned home from the war.

Elder Cliff Hampton, an Old Regular Baptist minister and close friend of I.D., recalled during an interview with this author that, even in those days, when he was a sinner partaking of liquor, I.D. "had the voice of an angel." Hampton would recall hearing stories of I.D., during his days as a coal truck driver, jumping upon heaps of coal and beautifully singing hymns. Hampton also remembers that I.D. continued to mimic the preaching of Old Regular Baptist sermons at this time.

Sadly, Elder Hampton himself passed away just prior to the publication of this book.

During his years of sin, I.D. encountered several individuals who would become lifelong friends and supporters. One of these men was Ray Back. When presented with a question regarding where he first met I.D. Back, Ray Back recalls that their initial meeting probably occurred in Goebel Stamp's Place, sometime after the end of WW II. Oddly enough, one would have expected that the two gentlemen would have encountered each other prior to this time. There was some relation between their families. Both of the young men were from Letcher County. Both fought in WWII. Still, it wasn't until after they'd returned from the war and met in Stamp's that they became well-acquainted with each other.

Ray and I.D. eventually formed a strong bond that would, as was previously mentioned, last a lifetime. In years to come, they would sometimes find themselves involved in mischief together.

Ray recalls one time when he and I.D. were out together. On this particular occasion, the two decided that they wanted to buy beer. The selling of alcoholic beverages was, and still is, prohibited in Letcher County, and so they could not purchase liquor near home. In neighboring Perry County, however, such was not the case. Hence, the two decided to travel to Vicco (which is located in Perry County) to buy the booze that they were craving.

By this time, I.D. had acquired a job at an auto parts store. Because of his connections to the store, he was able to acquire a special horn for his car. Upon being tooted, the car's horn would play the tune of "Mary Had a Little Lamb."

In I.D.'s car, which sported the "Mary had a Little Lamb" horn, he and Ray traveled toward Vicco. After purchasing the liquor in Vicco, they traveled back toward Letcher County. They had just re-entered the county of Letcher and were traveling down a steep hill that locals know today as Garner Mountain. I.D. was at the wheel, and Ray remembers that the car was "absolutely flying."

Always a bit of a daredevil, I.D. was pressing his foot hard against the gas pedal, while his frightened passenger clung tightly to the seat of the car. Suddenly, the car hit a bump in the road which, Ray estimates, caused it to jump the width of a house. Poor Ray was terrified, but young I.D. remained unaffected. "Uh-oh, Ray!" he cheerfully exclaimed, "We've hit a air pocket!"

Later, he would take a job at Wardrup's Meat Packing Plant, which was located approximately three-fourths of a mile above the Blackey Bridge. No matter the job that I.D. undertook, he seemed to find humor in some of his daily experiences. In later years, he would relay to my father the story of one particularly funny incident that occurred during the time he worked at Wardrup's. This story involved my father's maternal uncle, Chester "Dick" Bailey.

Dick was a lifelong bachelor, who immensely enjoyed partaking of alcoholic beverages. He was a simple man, who was very small in stature (approximately 5-feet-tall). While I can barely remember him now (as I was very young when he died), I'm told that he did have one spectacular gift in life...he was hilarious!

Because of Dick's ability to entertain and make others laugh, I.D. would often pick him up and haul him around in the company truck during the workday. One day, Dick did something that I.D. found particularly entertaining, and, after he told the story to Dad in later years, Dad would recount it again and again with gales of laughter. It seems that, on this particular occasion, Dick was riding in the passenger seat of the company truck. After riding for a while, he asked if I.D. would mind if he stretched a bit. Thinking that Dick simply meant that he was going to raise his arms above his head and stretch, I.D. responded that he, of course, did not mind. It was at this point, however, that Dick surprised him. He did raise his arms above his head in a stretch, but he did not do so while he was resting in the passenger seat. Instead, he proceeded to stand up in the truck first, and then he stretched. Not many people would have been short enough to perform this task, and I.D. would laughingly recount this story to others for years to come.

Other jobs that I.D. would hold throughout his life included, but were not limited to, the following: driver of a bread truck, store clerk, and store owner. There will be further discussion of some of these jobs, as well as some of I.D.'s other jobs, throughout the remainder of this book.

However, at this point, we're going to begin discussion of a very important decision that I.D. made at the time that he was working at the auto parts store. It was during this time in his life that he decided that he had already met the woman with whom he wanted to spend the rest of his life, and he was going to ask her to marry him.

CHAPTER 8
Courtship and Marriage

Petite in frame, with a dark complexion, nearly-black eyes, and raven hair reminiscent of her Cherokee heritage, the lovely Miss Ina Rose Hamilton had spent much of her childhood outside the confines of Kentucky. Although she was born in this state, as the last of four daughters born to Arch and Susan Combs Hamilton, she moved to Tennessee as a child.

While her mother was carrying her in the womb, tragic news came to the Hamilton home. Arch, a small man, who family members recall presented with mild signs of "being crippled," had been badly injured in a mining accident that had occurred during his usual work day. He was not dead, but his neck had been broken.

Young Susan was undoubtedly heartsick. Aside from worrying that this man, whom she had loved for so many years, would die and leave her a widow, she had children to consider. What would happen to the three little girls that she and Arch were currently raising? What about the little baby that had not yet arrived, but was on the way? One can only imagine the hours of worry and prayer that filled her days and nights during the period following Arch's accident.

Alas, however, Mr. Hamilton was not meant to recover. He developed pneumonia while bedridden, and he died from complications of that pneumonia.

A short time after Arch Hamilton's death, On October 28, 1928, the baby that Susan had been expecting at the time of his death would enter the world with wails. Susan called the new baby Ina Rose.

While young Ina Rose never had the opportunity to know her father, she was not without love in her life.

Her mother, as well as her older sisters Mable, Elizabeth ("Tootsie"), and Virginia ("Jenny"), showered her with affection during her childhood years.

A bit of a tomboy, Ina Rose enjoyed engaging in sporting events. While attending elementary school in Tennessee, she was a member of the basketball team. In fact, Ronnie recalls hearing people say, in later years, that his mother had been very skilled in this sport.

Upon her completion of elementary school, Ina Rose and her family moved back to Kentucky. At that point, she was enrolled as a student at Stuart Robinson High School. Unfortunately, this school did not have a girls' basketball team. Needless to say, this did not please the athletic Miss Hamilton. To pacify her, school officials allowed her to serve as a referee at boys' basketball games.

Perhaps the fact that she had spent much of her childhood in Tennessee would explain why Ina Rose Hamilton and I.D. Back had never met prior to his first furlough from the army in 1943. I.D. would later remember entering C.B. Caudill's Store and seeing this raven-haired beauty with her friend, Josephine Branson. He was instantly attracted to her. He would recall in an interview with this author, that, prior to that point, he had not known that "such as that was in the world."

The attraction was mutual. Ina Rose would later recall whispering to her girlfriend, "Jo, Who's that?!"

"That's I.D. Back," Josephine replied.

"Well," Ina Rose responded, "He's mine if I never get him!"

The two, according to I.D.'s recollections, did not make plans for a date at that initial meeting. After they had parted ways, however, he kept thinking about her, and, later that evening, fearful that she would find someone else to love and he would never see her again, I.D. managed to find Ina Rose again and ask her out for a date.

In those days, the train depot was a popular spot among young gentlemen and ladies who were engaged in courtship. Hence, it was at that location that I.D. Back and Ina Rose Hamilton would have their first date. With a twinkle in his eyes, I.D. would later recount that he had jerked a handkerchief out of his pocket and used it to wipe clean a spot on a bench, so that Ina Rose would not have to sit on a dirty seat. After she sat down on the newly-cleaned bench, I.D. pulled a French harp from his other pocket and began serenading her there at the train depot. It was at this point in time that a very special relationship began...a relationship that would, in later years, be described by their son as "a fairy-tale romance."

After his initial meeting with Ina Rose, I.D.'s furlough ended, and he had to return to military duty. During the years that passed between that initial meeting and I.D.'s discharge from the army, the mail carriers likely delivered hundreds of letters in which the two corresponded.

Phyllis Asher, a friend and neighbor who often helped I.D. and Ina Rose with household chores during their latter years, would later recall Ina Rose reminiscing to her about how handsome I.D. had looked, as a youth, in his uniform!

After I.D.'s discharge from the army, his courtship with Ina Rose continued. She had undoubtedly haunted his thoughts and dreams during the time that he was away at war, and it is very likely that, at times, he had wondered if he would ever get to see her again. Thus, now that he was back in Blackey, Ina Rose would be seeing a great deal of him.

As was stated in an earlier chapter, I.D. had initially hoped, upon returning from the war, to complete his education. During this brief stint in which he had returned to school, family friend Clell Cornett would carry letters back and forth between I.D. and Ina Rose.

During her courtship with I.D., Ina Rose endured a great deal! Despite the fact that she was the love of his life, even she was not immune to his pranks and antics. Elder Elwood Cornett would, on the day of Ina Rose's funeral, recall a story that his brother Clell had told him. As the story told, I.D., Ina Rose, and Clell were one day traveling down the road in an A-model car. I.D. was driving, while Ina Rose was seated in the middle, and Clell was seated on the passenger side, next to the window. After a while, I.D. decided that he no longer wanted to drive. Instead, he wanted to move to the passenger seat, so that he could be closer to Ina Rose. Because of this, he suggested that Clell should drive for a while. Rather than pulling the car off the road and trading places with Clell, however, I.D. climbed out the window of the moving car and pulled himself over the top of the vehicle and through the passenger-side window. Meanwhile, Clell climbed over Ina Rose and slid into the driver's seat! For a brief instant, poor Ina Rose must have feared that her life was going to end as the result of a terrible car wreck!

Alas, however, the threesome did survive that incident, and I.D. and Ina Rose went on to have other dates. During one of their dates, I.D. turned to Ina Rose and said, "Do you like fried chicken, Ina Rose?" When she responded that, indeed, she did like fried chicken, he offered her his arm, so that he might escort her, and said, "Okay. Take a wing!"

One evening, they were parked at a coal tipple "sparking" (i.e., on a date), and it was here that I.D. Back would ask Ina Rose Hamilton if she would be his wife. Despite his antics, she loved him, and she accepted his marriage proposal.

On June 20, 1947, the two were married by Elder Kennell Sexton at the home of Clyde Caudill. Despite the fact that Ina Rose was 18-years-old at the time of the marriage, Sherry Back Fugate remembers her mother recounting the story and saying that she had needed a note from her own mother in order to wed I.D. at that age. So, Ina Rose had gotten a friend to write a letter giving her permission to marry, and the friend had forged Susan Hamilton's name. When this author went to view the marriage license at the Letcher County Court House, there was indication that a note from the parent had been attached. Witnesses to the marriage were listed as follows: Clyde Caudill, Margaret Lusk, and Lester Lusk.

After the wedding ceremony, the newlyweds climbed into I.D.'s car and embarked upon a honeymoon trip that would take them to Renfro Valley, Kentucky. Along the way, they stopped and visited Dog Patch Trading Post in London, Kentucky. Being the fun-loving person that he was, it's likely that I.D. tooted the "Mary had a Little Lamb" horn several times along the way.

At the end of the honeymoon, the two returned to Blackey, Kentucky. That is where they had met and courted. Now, it was where they would spend their life as husband and wife.

C. B. Caudill Store-the site of I.D.'s initial meeting with Ina Rose Hamilton. (Author's personal collection)

CHAPTER 9
Married...But Not Quite Settled Down

Along Highway Seven, there is a row of houses located between the home where I.D. and Ina Rose spent their latter years together and the C.B. Caudill Store. One of these houses, a small, white house with a big porch and banisters, would eventually become the home of Crittie Andrews. A tiny lady with silver hair, Crittie lived well into her nineties and maintained a sharp mind until just a few months before she died. Friends and neighbors loved her, and practically everyone in the area referred to her as Aunt Crittie. As the sister of I.D.'s mother, however, she truly was I.D.'s aunt.

Before Aunt Crittie lived in the house, however, it belonged to I.D. and Ina Rose. That is the house that the newlyweds moved into in 1947.

Just over a year after their marriage, Ina Rose gave birth to the couple's first child. A dark-haired baby boy with a dark complexion and nearly-black eyes, this child bore a strong resemblance to his mother. The young couple called him Ronald Wakefield. His middle name was given in honor of I.D.'s nephew and high school chum, Wakefield Back.

Despite the fact that he was now married and had a young son, however, I.D. Back was not yet finished "sowing his oats." Ronnie Back recalls one story that he had heard repeatedly over the years. This story involved I.D. and Walt Back, and it occurred at a time when tension was high among those involved in the mining industry.

The head of the UMW (United Mine Workers) was John L. Lewis. Ronnie remembers that, even though the war was now over, Walt and I.D. had still neither forgotten nor forgiven the fact that, during the war, Mr. Lewis had called a strike. This strike had affected energy supply nationwide in a country that was already suffering from rationing and other effects of World War II. As men who were very patriotic themselves, Walt and I.D. had found such action to be incomprehensible at the time of its occurrence. Thus, when the strike had ended and the young Backs had returned to Blackey, they found an opportunity to publicly express their displeasure with Mr. Lewis.

As the story goes, Walt and I.D. became intoxicated quite frequently. However, on this particular occasion, they, during their drunken states, began to dwell on thoughts of Mr. Lewis and his action, which had seemed so atrocious to them. As they continued to drink, they continued to ponder this action. The more they thought, and the more they drank, the angrier the two became. Finally, they became so angry that, in this moment of intoxication, they felt it necessary for them to go to a local coal tipple and speak their piece about the matter.

Upon arrival at the tipple, they shouted, "Are any of you all John L. Lewis supporters?" Some of the men at the tipple stepped forward and stated that, indeed, they were supporters of Mr. Lewis. At this point, words were exchanged between these men and the Back brothers. Soon, levels of agitation became so high that a brawl ensued between the Back Brothers and some of those men who had expressed support for Mr. Lewis.

By the time the brawl was stopped, many friends and family members believed it unsafe for Walt and I.D. to remain in Blackey. So, fearing for their safety, their brother Bill, who was a foreman at the mine, gave them some money and told them to get out of the county for a while. With money in tow, the two young brothers hopped on a train and headed for some location far away from Blackey. Ronnie Back believes that they went to Cincinnati.

When they reached their destination, they immediately searched for the best motel they could find (as the funding for their stay was coming from money that had been given to them, and not from money that they had actually had to work to earn). When it came time for them to sign the hotel registry, Walt grabbed the book from I.D. and signed their names as follows: Frank and Jesse Back.

For a brief time, the two brothers enjoyed themselves immensely. After staying at the hotel for just a short period of time, however, they realized that, in buying liquor and good food, they had squandered most of their money and now had very little left. In fact, they did not even have enough money to pay for a return trip to Blackey.

A niece, Margaret Bracken, lived in a nearby county. It was she who came to their rescue at this point. She paid their hotel bill, and then took them back to her home for a brief stay. They resided with their niece, until such point that it was considered safe for them to return to Blackey.

CHAPTER 10
God Has Mercy on I.D.'s Soul

Indeed, as stories already recounted will evidence, I.D. drank a great deal of liquor during his sinful days. In fact, it was his infamous tendency to partake of liquor in those years that could be held accountable for how it came to be that, on a warm, summer night in 1951, he found himself seated on a bar stool, in a Hazard, Kentucky night club known as The Chat'N Chew. Just as the case had been on many similar nights in his past, a beer-filled mug rested on the counter in front of him.

This night was different from past nights in one very important way, however. When I.D. Back raised that mug to his lips, he underwent an experience that he had not undergone on past nights in the bar. He became overwhelmed by a sudden sense of sadness, and, in that instant, he began to reflect upon the life that he had lived prior to this point. He thought about his sinful acts, and he likely pondered on how the sinful lifestyle that he was now living was so far from the Christian lifestyle that his parents had lived. His current sinful lifestyle gave no evidence to the fact that he had been raised in a home where, from the day of his birth, Christian values were instilled in him. He would remember in later years that, at this point, a voice in his head said, "Are you going to drink that?" It was then that he lowered the mug back to its previous resting place on the counter, without taking a drink of the liquor that it held. Then, he walked out of the bar.

That is not to say that I.D. obtained salvation in The Chat'N Chew, for that was not the case. This bar just happened to be the location in which he was seated when he decided that he needed to start striving to obtain salvation. It was in that bar that he decided that he needed to change his lifestyle and seek God.

He went home, and he went to bed. Sleep, however, was not to encompass him on that night. His conscience was haunting him too much for sleep to come. He knew that he was a sinner. He also knew, as his parents had taught him, that he would eventually die and go to Hell, UNLESS God decided to show him mercy and forgive him of his sins. As he lay there on that night, he prayed that God would save his soul. That was not the night that God saved him, though.

The worry and prayers would continue throughout the week to come. Alas, I.D. became so weary and so scared of death and eternal damnation in Hell that he prayed fervently, "God, if You got any more mercy, PLEASE let it come!" He would recall in later years that, at that moment (one week after he had set the beer-filled mug back on the counter at the Hazard bar), as he lay on his back in his bed, with Ina Rose on one side of him and young Ronnie on the other side, God saved his soul. He would recall that, in the instant that God saved his soul, he felt as if a bolt of lightning had stricken the top of his head, traveled all the way down his body, and "shot out" through the soles of his feet. This feeling was followed by a sense of calm and well-being.

The author, at this point, will note that, after talking with several individuals who have obtained salvation, she has learned that everyone has not had the same experience of salvation that I.D. Back had. While I.D. recalled a feeling similar to that of a lightning bolt's strike, others have reported that, at the moment their sins were forgiven, they experienced an all-encompassing feeling of peace and well-being. Salvation is a personal experience between an individual and God. Thus, the experience of salvation is not the same for everybody. The author states this simply for the purpose of clarification, so that any reader who is currently seeking salvation will not feel that he has not obtained salvation until such point that he feels that lightning bolt hit his body.

Salvation came to I.D. on Saturday night. On the following Sunday morning, he was seated in a pew near the rear section of a church atop a hill near the "Frog Pond." (The "Frog Pond" is an area that's located approximately one mile north of the Blackey Bridge. This author is unsure as to how the area originally received this unusual name, but it can be described as a relatively swampy area that floods easily in the event that hard rains fall upon the region.)

The name of the church referred to above was the Indian Bottom Church at the Frog Pond. A small, white church, with a beautiful, tall steeple, this church continues to stand today. The building is still an occasional site for a church service. A sign at the bottom of the hill reads "Old Indian Bottom Church."

When one walks into this church, he immediately sees a middle aisle, with pews on each side. On the morning that I.D. had planned to join the church, Ina Rose was seated by his side on one of those pews, and he held young Ronnie in his arms.

As the service ended, members of the congregation stood and sang a song in unison, while the preacher "gave the invitation." This phrase("gave the invitation") refers to the preacher's standing and inviting anyone who feels that he/she has been saved to come to the front of the church and, in the words that I have heard uttered at the closing of so many Old Regular Baptist church services, "give your hand to the church and come into the church by experience and baptism."

I.D. would recall in later years that, as he stood at the pew, with his young son in his arms, his feet felt "as heavy as lead." Suddenly, though, he felt that he simply could not wait any longer. He had to join the church and let everyone there know that God had saved his soul. So, he handed the child to its mother, and put one of his feet out into the aisle. He would recall that, after he put that first foot forward, God did the rest. Before he knew it, he was running down the aisle of the church and falling into the outstretched arms of the husky preacher with reddish-brown hair who had closed the services on that day. (The preacher who "closes" the service is the last one to stand in the pulpit during a service.) The preacher's last name was Whitaker. (Ironically, I.D. would later say that, prior to this day, he had never seen this particular preacher and that, after this day, he never saw him again.)

As soon as she became aware that I.D. was joining the church, one woman began sobbing and shouting with joy, "My Baby! My Baby!" It was his mother. Just as she had cried for joy when God safely delivered him home from war, she was now crying for joy again, because, this time, God had rescued him from the grip of sin.

Elwood Cornett recalls being in the congregation on the day that I.D. Back joined the church. He remembers that, after I.D. had been "taken into the church" (process conducted by one male church member making a motion that the individual be received into the church and, then, another male church member saying that he seconds that motion) and given "the right hand of fellowship" (when each member of the congregation comes to the front of the church and hugs and/or shakes the hand of the new church member so that he will feel welcome among them), he returned to his wife in the crowd and bestowed a hug upon her. When he began to hug her, she leaned forward to embrace him, and, while leaning forward, lifted her foot up behind her. Elwood felt that this was reminiscent of actions taken by the actresses in old movies, and, as a youngster, he found this to be amusing.

On the third Sunday of August, in 1951, near the meat packing plant at which he would be employed in years to come, I.D. Back was lowered into Rock House Creek by the church's preacher, and baptized in the name of the Father, the Son, and the Holy Ghost.

As news of I.D.'s salvation spread throughout the community, there were various words of doubt and disbelief expressed by friends and neighbors who had known him for years. They knew that he drank. They knew that he was mischievous. They knew that he spent much of his time engaged in some sort of activity that would get him into trouble. One, upon hearing the good news, would say, "What?! I just saw him drunk last week!" Others would utter the prediction that, when told to church congregations in years to come, would bring smiles and chuckles. The prediction was as follows: "He won't last 30 days!"

It has been said that members of the community loved I.D., even during the time that he was a sinner. One friend has said that, even in his days of sin, I.D. was quick-witted, jolly, and friendly to all. How could they not love such a personable young man? Hence, it was not out of dislike that they uttered their expressions of doubt. They were uttering these statements simply because, based upon what they had always known of I.D. in the past, they believed these statements to be true. He truly had been seen in a drunken state just a few weeks prior to the time that he received salvation.

What his friends and neighbors did not yet know, but would soon find out, was this - I.D. Back was a changed man. Ray and Beulah Back would later recall noticing this change the first time that they returned from their home in Louisville for a visit to the mountains. While he had always been a friendly man, they remember that he was, after obtaining salvation, encompassed by a sense of humility ("humbleness," as I.D. would say).

When speaking of those who thought that his salvation had been obtained too quickly to be authentic, I.D. would say, "They don't know what I went through in that week!" By "that week," he was referring to the week that passed between the Saturday night that he set his beer down and walked out of a Hazard bar and the following Saturday night, on which God forgave him of his sins and saved his soul from eternal damnation in Hell.

The old Indian Bottom Church at the "Frog Pond"
This is the church at which I.D. Back initially had membership.
(Author's personal collection)

CHAPTER 11
Separate Classifications of Old Regular Baptists

At this point, it is important for the author to briefly explain the divisions among groups of Old Regular Baptists; otherwise, the reader might not understand why some of the events in I.D.'s life, that are yet to be discussed, took place as they did.

Divisions among the churches are referred to as "associations." Old Regular Baptists comprise a large group of people; however, while they all refer to themselves as Old Regular Baptists, they do not all belong to the same church association. There actually are several different associations of the Old Regular Baptist Church (e.g., Indian Bottom Association, Old Indian Bottom Association, Thornton Union Association, New Salem Association, Old Union Association).

While similar in many ways and supporters of basically the same church doctrine, the members of different associations also differ in some of their beliefs (e.g., appropriate apparel for church members). Hence, to avoid conflict and to avoid confusion among members of the congregations, preachers of different associations typically do not correspond with each other during the time that they are conducting church services. If a preacher from the Indian Bottom Association, for example, visits a church that is part of another association (e.g., Old Indian Bottom), he will not likely be invited to preach at the service that he is attending.

In later years, I.D. would be a member of a church that is part of the Indian Bottom Association. When he initially joined the church and was baptized, however, this was not the case. In the late 1920's, the Indian Bottom Church at the Frog Pond had seen a split among members of its congregation. Some of the members remained, but others chose to move to the Lower Indian

Bottom Church. (At that time, the Lower Indian Bottom Church was located on a hill between Caudill's Branch and the Blackey city limits. Now, it is located in the tiny community of Red Star.)

At the time of the split, the two halves that were involved in the dispute took their arguments before the leaders of their association. The association leaders sided with the Lower Indian Bottom Church. At that point, the few remaining members of the Indian Bottom Church at the Frog Pond were temporarily left without a preacher. That situation was remedied one day, however, when I.D.'s uncle came in contact with a man that was deemed suitable for the position.

Since that time, some people have speculated as to whether or not this man was of the Old Regular Baptist faith. That's not to say that there was speculation about his salvation or his desire to serve God. Those who were members of the church at the time, however, believed that he was of the same faith as they were. Because they were of this belief, and because they were in need of a preacher, it was decided that this man would be the new preacher at the Old Indian Bottom Church at the Frog Pond.

Hence, at the time that I.D. joined the church, this preacher was serving as the moderator of the church that he joined. (In many ways, a moderator is to a church or association what a president is to a country. He presides over business matters relative to the church or association that he moderates.) Furthermore, it was he who baptized I.D. These facts, coupled with the question of whether or not this man truly was of the Old Regular Baptist faith, would impact I.D. in years to come. After all, if the man who baptized him was not an Old Regular Baptist, then I.D. would be considered by members of other churches in other associations to not be an Old Regular Baptist. That, however, will be discussed in a later chapter.

Before moving on to the next chapter, the author should also explain that, within a particular association, there are several different churches that have their monthly meetings at the same time. Some churches (e.g., Mt. Olivet, Poor Fork, Kingdom Come) have their meeting times scheduled for the first Sunday of the month. Other churches (e.g., Little Zion, Little Dove, Defeated Creek) have their meeting times scheduled for the second Sunday of the month. On the third Sunday of the month, still other churches (e.g., Big Leatherwood, Blair Branch, Bull Creek, Hurricane Gap) have their meeting times scheduled. Then, on the fourth Sunday of the month, still more churches (e.g., Cedar Grove, Tolson Creek, Big Cowan) have meeting times scheduled. Then, if there happens to be an "odd weekend"(or 5th weekend) in the month, church services are generally held at the Indian Bottom Association Building (located in Yellow Creek, Kentucky). (Sometimes, members of one of the other churches may also opt to have a special "called meeting" at their church on an odd Sunday.)

Still, all of those churches mentioned above are in the same association (i.e., Indian Bottom Association). Hence, Old Regular Baptists "belonging to" (or having membership at) any church within the Indian Bottom Association may choose to go to any of the church services being held on a given weekend. Church members have a home church (where they take their "letter" or membership upon initially joining the church), and they generally go to that home church when services are being held there. That is not always the case, however. Sometimes, members will leave their home church one month to attend services at another church within their association. Then, on the Sundays that services are not being held at their home church, members will choose, from the churches that are holding services on those Sundays, which church they want to attend.

This is true of Old Regular Baptist preachers, also. They do not preach only at their home church. They preach at various churches throughout their respective association.

CHAPTER 12
A Calling to the Ministry

Those familiar with the ways of the Old Regular Baptist Church know that its ministers, as was stated in an earlier chapter, are not required to obtain training at a seminary. In fact, they are not required to have any education at all. The only qualification needed for a man to become an Old Regular Baptist preacher is this - he must feel "the calling." (Note that the author said that was the only qualification needed for a man. It is the belief of Old Regular Baptist Church members that only men will be called to preach.) In other words, if a male church member feels that God wants him to become a preacher, he is thought to be feeling "the calling."

My own father is an Old Regular Baptist minister, and he has told me that it is a very fearful thing when a man feels "the calling" to the ministry. One often has to endure a period of travail before telling the moderator of his home church that he feels he's called to preach and would like to make "an offering" at the next church service. (In this case, an "offering" refers to the preacher's willingness to stand in the pulpit and attempt to preach a sermon, while having faith that God will bless him to do so).

Recently, I asked my father to provide for me a description of what "the calling" feels like. He began his response by saying, "First of all, the greatest thing that ever happened to a man or a woman is to be born again." He went on to say that sinners who are in the process of confessing their sins to God and asking Him for forgiveness are not likely to be worried, at that point, about whether of not they are called to preach. It is my father's opinion that being called to preach would likely be the farthest thing from the mind of a sinner who is trying to obtain salvation. He stated that the main concern of these sinners would be that they get forgiveness of their sins and become Christians. As Dad said, "You can't be 'called', until you're a Christian."

He summed up the meaning of the message that he had been trying to convey to me with the following words: "God calls men that's born again. Men don't join the church to become preachers. The calling comes after that."

My father did go on to say, however, that, while men do not join the church for the purpose of becoming preachers, God does have the ability to see into the future, and He knows who He will call in the future to become a preacher. Thus, it is Dad's belief that "all true, genuine preachers, who are called of God, are chosen vessels."

He states, when speaking of Old Regular Baptists' beliefs about preachers, "We don't believe that (just) anybody can preach. There has to be a calling...a Heavenly, Divine calling." Then, he used scripture to support this belief. He explained that, when Jesus was speaking to Ananais about Saul (who was later called Paul), Jesus said, "Go thy way: for he is a chosen vessel unto me, to bear my name before the Gentiles, and kings, and the children of Israel" (Acts 9:15). Reference was also made to Romans 10:14 and 10:15, which state, "How then shall they call on him in whom they have not believed? and how shall they believe in Him of whom they have not heard? and how shall they hear without a preacher? and how shall they preach, except they be sent? As it is written, HOW BEAUTIFUL ARE THE FEET OF THEM THAT PREACH THE GOSPEL OF PEACE, AND BRING GLAD TIDINGS OF GOOD THINGS."

My father went on to say that this calling comes as "a deep conviction or a sincere, overwhelming constrained spirit, or a feeling of constrainment, to warn men and women to flee from the wrath to come...to flee from the eternal terror (and) catastrophic punishment of everlasting fire and brimstone and agony and pain and gnashing of teeth - where the smoke of men's and women's torments will ascend up forever- where there'll be no rest, day or night." In order to further emphasize the severity of the torments that would await these unrepentant sinners who those called to preach feel constrained to warn, he referred to 2nd Thessalonians 1:7-1:9, which reads, "...when the Lord Jesus shall be revealed from Heaven with his mighty angels, in flaming fire taking vengeance on them that know not God, and that obey not the gospel of our Lord Jesus Christ: who shall be punished with everlasting destruction from the presence of the Lord, and from the glory of his power."

Dad, however, also said, "Even with the conviction we feel and this overwhelming, constraining feeling, we hesitate, and we are very hesitant about rushing into it (preaching)....Preaching the gospel is something not to be taken, or entered into, lightly. It's something that's most serious, and it's a fearful undertaking." When questioned about why this is such a fearful undertaking, he replied, "'Cause we believe that, when someone stands in the presence of God to preach the Gospel, to proclaim the Gospel...it's a holy place (in which) that we stand." He further stated, "We believe you NEED to make the calling as sure as you can...."

"And then, after the deep conviction and the constraining spirit and the fear and the feeling that God has called you, you come to a point where you're afraid to try (to preach) and afraid not to, because you fear God. There comes a point in your life that, if God's called you, there'll be no peace within you, until you're obedient to that calling. And then, when you become obedient to that calling with much fearfulness, sincerity, and humbleness...then there's a DESIRE that sets up inside of a man...." At this point, my tenderhearted father was overtaken by spiritual joy, and he began to cry. After regaining his composure somewhat, he continued saying, "to preach the gospel of Jesus Christ. That (desire to preach the Gospel) is brought by a mighty, powerful force called the Spirit of God - the Holy Ghost. With that desire comes a - something that's really grounded and settled - determination and will to preach in such a manner to please God, to always please God, and not man. When you become obedient and have this desire (to preach the Gospel), you become as Paul." At this point, he supported his beliefs by referring to Romans 1:15 and 1:16 in which Paul says to the Romans, "So, as much as in me is, I am ready to preach the gospel to you that are at Rome, also. For I am not ashamed of the gospel of Christ: for it is the power of God unto salvation to everyone that believeth...."

Author's father, Danny Dixon, stands in his yard with
I.D.Back.
(Personal Collection of Danny and Teresa Dixon)

CHAPTER 13
Expectations for Old Regular Baptist Ministers

What is expected of a minister in the Old Regular Baptist church? Again, I turned to my father for assistance in answering this question. He responded, "We believe that those who preach the Gospel should live of the Gospel." In other words, as the old adage proclaims, they're expected to "practice what they preach."

My father stated, "We also believe that they are to speak that which becomes sound doctrine and those who are called are expected to labor in the Word and in the doctrine by studying the Bible, and to give attendance to reading, exhortation, and doctrine to meditate upon these things." When I asked him if there was a scripture that would support this, he responded, "Yes, there is. I wouldn't say it if there wasn't, and don't you swallow it if there ain't!"

At this point, he referred me to the second chapter of Titus, in which Paul writes to Titus, "But speak thou the things which become sound doctrine" (Titus 2:1).

He also made reference to the 1st book of Timothy, in which Paul tells Timothy, "...give attendance to reading, to exhortation, to doctrine. ...Meditate upon these things; give thyself wholly to them; that thy profiting may appear to all. Take heed unto thyself, and unto the doctrine; continue in them: for in doing this thou shalt both save thyself and them that hear thee" (Timothy 4:13, 4:15, and 4:16).

Finally, to further support the need for ministers to study the Word of God, he made reference to a scripture that reads, "Study to show thyself approved unto God..." (2nd Timothy 2:15).

What about the ministers who are illiterate? God does make a way. He does perform miracles. If a preacher cannot read the Bible, God will provide some way of allowing him to get the information that he needs to get from the Bible. Perhaps someone will read the Bible to him. He may even listen to the Bible as it is read over audio tapes.

My father is a classic example of the way in which God performs miracles. He was a poor student in school. This was not because he wasn't intelligent, but simply because he would have rather bounced a basketball than read a book. It was difficult for him to sit and concentrate on his studies for long periods of time. Since God has called him to preach, however, he has been blessed to be able to study his Bible and understand the meaning of verses therein. He has also been blessed with an amazing ability to remember and recite Biblical scriptures. The moral of this story? Man does not preach on the basis of his natural abilities. He is able to preach only when God blesses him to do so. Furthermore, if it's God's will that a man preach, then He will bless that man to overcome the natural weaknesses that might hinder him in this endeavor.

Dad further stated, in regard to what Old Regular Baptists expect of their ministers, "We believe that, when God calls us, we are to abide in the calling wherein He had called us." In support of this statement, he referred to the book of 1st Corinthians. Within this book of the Bible, Paul wrote to the Corinthians, "Let every man abide in the same calling wherein he was called. Art thou called being a servant? care not for it: but if thou mayest be made free, use it rather. For he that is called in the Lord, being a servant, is the Lord's freeman: likewise also he that is called, being free, is Christ's servant. Ye are bought with a price; be not ye the servants of men. Brethren, let every man, wherein he is called, therein abide with God" (1st Corinthians 7:20-24).

He elaborated by saying, "We don't believe that there are MANY wise or noble people who are called - stress that the Bible says 'not many' NOT 'not any.' The Bible says that He gives people several talents according to their abilities." The verse to which he is referring states, "And unto one he gave five talents, to another two, and to another one; to every man according to his several ability..." (Matthew 25:15).

In other words, those whom God has called to preach have been blessed by God to have different talents. Perhaps one is blessed with the gift to sing beautifully. Another may be blessed with the gift of remembering and interpreting the meaning of Biblical verses. Still others may be blessed with the ability to act as counselors to members of the congregation. Some ministers, such as I.D. Back, have been given multiple talents.

My father further stated that, after God bestows a talent or talents upon someone, "He uses them according to the abilities that He's given them." Whatever a minister's talent(s) may be, God expects that individual to use the talent(s) with which he's been blessed for the purpose of drawing lost sinners unto repentance and salvation.

This is supported by Biblical verse. Before Jesus ascended back into Heaven, he told his disciples that it was needful for him to go back to Heaven, but that he would pray to the Father, and the Father would send them a Comforter, the Holy Ghost. For elaboration, refer to the book of John, where Jesus is quoted as saying, "But the Comforter, which is the Holy Ghost, whom the Father will send in my name, he shall teach you all things, and bring all things to your remembrance, whatsoever I have said unto you" (John 14:26).

One way in which Old Regular Baptist ministers differ from ministers of many other faiths is this - they do not take money for the provision of services relative to their ministerial duties. In the words of my father, "Freely we receive the gospel, and freely we give it away." Occasionally, if one of the ministers travels a great distance to a church that's located out of state, someone at the church might offer to give him money for gas. Sometimes, there truly is a situation in which dire need is present, and, in these cases, God will provide. More often than not, however, the minister will refuse even to take money that would cover the cost of his gas for the trip.

The belief against taking money for services rendered in the name of God is supported by a Bible verse from the book of Matthew. In this book of the Bible, it is recorded that Christ said unto his apostles, "But go rather to the lost sheep of the house of Israel. And as ye go, preach, saying, The kingdom of Heaven is at hand. Heal the sick, cleanse the lepers, raise the dead: freely ye have received, freely give" (Matthew 10: 6-8).

Additional backing of this belief can be found in the 1st book of Corinthians. In this book, Paul writes to the Corinthians, "What is my reward then? Verily that, when I preach the gospel, I may make the gospel of Christ without charge, that I abuse not my power in the gospel" (1st Corinthians 9:18).

Further support comes from the book of 1st Peter. Within this book, it is stated, "Feed the flock of God which is among you, taking the oversight thereof, not by constraint, but willingly; not for filthy lucre, but of a ready mind" (1st Peter 5:2). In the book of 1st Peter, it is also written, "And when the chief Shepherd shall appear, ye shall receive a crown of glory that fadeth not away" (1st Peter 5:4).

Thus, Old Regular Baptist ministers base their belief that they should not take money for performing God's work on the scriptures mentioned on the previous page. In short, they are of the belief that their jobs as servants of God will be rewarded, in the end, when they meet face-to-face with the Lord Jesus Christ.

Another attribute of Old Regular Baptist ministers, which differs from that of ministers in other denominations, is related to preparation of sermons. Quite simply, Old Regular Baptist ministers do not do this. As was already stated, they do study their Bibles throughout the course of the week, and, occasionally, they might consider what they'd like to say about a given topic (in the event that the Lord blesses them to do so). However, they do not write sermons out ahead of time. They step into the pulpit as willing speakers for God. At that point, they believe that their ability to preach is dependent upon God's blessing. If He blesses a preacher on that day, then He will provide that preacher with a topic to preach about, and He will allow that preacher to recall the information from the Bible that pertains to the topic at hand.

Finally, my father stated that it is expected that ministers of God will be "willing to spend and be spent - to labor for the Lord. To be persecuted (and) reviled. (They're) willing to stand as necessary." Again, he used Biblical verse in support of these expectations. Within the book of Corinthians, Paul writes, "For though I be free from all men, yet have I made myself servant unto all, that I might gain the more. And unto the Jews I became as a Jew, that I might gain the Jews; to them that are under the law, as under the law, that I might gain them that are under the law; To them are without law, as without law, (being not without law to God, but under the law to Christ), that I might gain them that are without law; To the weak became I as weak, that I might gain the weak: I am made all things to all men, that I might by all means save some. And this I do for the gospel's sake..." (1st Corinthians 9:19-23).

In simple terms, this author deduced that the expectations for Old Regular Baptist ministers are as follows: (1) They're expected to practice the virtues that they preach to others; (2) They're expected to study their Bibles and meditate upon the Biblical verses that they have read; and (3) They're expected to spend their lives, no matter the personal cost, ministering freely to others and doing whatever they can do, using the talents that God has given them, to lead lost sinners unto repentance.

Upon later review of this list, however, the author's father stated that there is one more expectation for an Old Regular Baptist preacher. He is expected to serve as a preacher, until such point that poor health or death prevents him from doing so. In the words of my father, "they never retire." (The author's mother recalled one minister who carried an oxygen tank to church with him!)

Did I.D. fulfill the expectations for an Old Regular Baptist minister? Did he do all of the things mentioned above? These questions will be reflected upon in subsequent chapters.

Elder Back, along with other ministers and members of the church congregation, is pictured here at a memorial service in Red Star.
(Personal Collection of Danny and Teresa Dixon)

CHAPTER 14
I.D. Becomes A Preacher

Just a few months after he had joined the church, young I.D. Back began feeling "the calling" to the ministry. He was in the midst of a travail regarding this matter, and he had not yet informed anyone of his belief that he may be called to preach, when, one Sunday morning in the summer of 1952, he ventured out to a memorial service in a cemetery that was located atop a hill at the Letcher and Knott county lines. (In this case, a memorial service is a church service held at or near a cemetery for the purpose of honoring the individuals buried there. Regular church-goers, as well as family members of the people buried in the cemetery, generally attend these services. The services are generally held outside, and they are often followed by a potluck dinner or lunch.) Upon arriving at the memorial service, I.D. walked among the congregation until he found a seat in the midst of the crowd. He did not sit on the stand, where preachers typically sit. Nevertheless, when it was time for the service to begin, a preacher stood up and pointed at I.D., while admonishing the crowd that "this young fellar here's going to introduce today's services."

I.D. would recall in later years that he felt a sense of panic at that moment. He had definitely not expected to be invited to preach on this occasion, for, as was stated above, he had not even told anyone that he had felt a calling to the ministry. How could this preacher know what I.D. had felt in his heart?

At any rate, I.D. did feel "the calling," and this preacher had invited him to make an offering. Hence, the small man with the wavy, brown hair walked nervously to the front of the congregation and entered the pulpit. Once there, he would remember drawing a blank. He had no idea of what he would say to the congregation. Blank and fearful, he uttered the prayer, "Lord, please help me." At that moment, he remembered the 1st verse from the 8th chapter of Romans. This verse reads, "There is therefore no condemnation to them which are in Christ Jesus, who walk not after the flesh, but after the Spirit." Hence, that is the verse around which his first sermon revolved.

Elwood Cornett was in attendance at the memorial service on that day, and, hence, he was able to hear I.D.'s initial offering as a preacher. He would later recall that it was a short sermon, typical of those delivered by beginning preachers.

Elder Cornett was only a young boy of 14- or 15-years-old, when I.D. began preaching. Still, he has many memories relative to that time in I.D.'s life. He remembers, for example, that the Cornett family owned an old car that had cost around $200, and that he would transport his mother and father to church services, so that he would have an opportunity to drive the family car. For a young boy who had not yet reached the age of 16, this would have been quite a thrill!

On the way to the church service, the Cornett family would pass the house of Callie Back. She continued to live in her old home place, which was located atop a bank that was approximately one and one-half miles away from the Cornetts' home. As Callie had no car of her own, the Cornetts would often give her a ride to church. Elwood recalls slowly driving along the winding River Road that led from his house to the city of Blackey. As neither the Cornetts nor Callie Back had a telephone at that time, there was no way to call ahead and alert Callie that they were on their way to pick her up for church services. So, as the Cornett car rounded the curve, approximately one-half mile above Callie's home, Elwood would begin blowing the car horn in order to alert her of their impending arrival.

When the Cornett car drew to a stop in front of the Back home, Callie would come to the door and say, "Give me just a minute." They would all wait for her to walk down to the car. When she reached the car, she would crawl into the back seat and sit next to Elwood's mother, her good friend Artie Cornett. Elwood's father, Arch Cornett, would sit in front, next to him. Once they were all situated in their usual sitting spots, the car would pull away, and the four of them would travel toward the church service of choice for that day.

There were times that both Callie Back and Artie Cornett had difficulty walking up hills in order to reach some of the memorial services at which I.D. would be preaching. So, as a means of assistance, they would cling to Elwood's belt. Callie would hold one side of the belt, and Artie would hold the other side, as Elwood proceeded to walk up the hill, thereby pulling them along with him.

No doubt the efforts that I.D.'s mother went to in order to hear her son preach were rewarded. I.D. quickly became one of the most well-respected preachers in the mountains of Southeastern Kentucky.

CHAPTER 15
The Establishment of Mount Olivet Old Regular Baptist Church

As I.D.'s success as a preacher continued to increase, it has been speculated that some jealousy arose toward him. Other members of the Old Regular Baptist faith would not preach with him, because, technically, they did not consider him to be an Old Regular Baptist. The controversy about this can be traced back, in part, to the question involving whether or the man who baptized I.D., and moderated the church at which he preached, was an Old Regular Baptist.

The church at the Frog Pond was beginning to experience dissent among its members.

One Saturday, Elwood drove his parents by I.D.'s house, so that they could pick him up and take him to Saturday morning church services. Ina Rose came to the door of the house and informed the Cornetts that I.D. had gone to another church on this particular day. Furthermore, she informed them that I.D. had stated that he had no plans of ever returning to the church at the Frog Pond.

The Cornetts went on to Saturday morning church services without I.D. On this particular morning, the dissent of the members in this church was evident. At this meeting, some upsetting events that, at this time, are best left unmentioned, had occurred. As a result, most of I.D.'s supporters had already left the building and begun walking home. Fiercely loyal to I.D., however, one member of the congregation simply could not bear the idea that the young Preacher Back was being spoken of in an unflattering manner. Hence, at the meeting that morning, some words were exchanged, and the moderator invited this particular member to step outside with him so that the matter could be settled. The member agreed to this challenge, and, on his way out the door, he picked up a poker that was resting near the door. He reportedly did this in an attempt to even the odds, as everyone else who was still present in the building was in support of the moderator. Seeing the man grab the poker, the moderator decided that he no longer wanted to fight. The remaining members went home.

This happened many years ago. This author was not yet even born, and, hence, was certainly not in attendance at this meeting. So, the above account is based on the testimony of someone who was close to the action at that time. The reader should remember that neither I.D.Back nor the man who was serving as the church's moderator nor the church member who grabbed the poker is alive to give an account of the story. Hence, no disrespect is intended toward any of the parties involved in this disagreement.

Actually, the author finds this story to be very amusing, for this would most likely never happen in one of today's church services. This problem simply resulted from a lot of built-up anger and resentment. There was a lot of controversy at this time. Church business is discussed at Saturday services, and, when the business issues were addressed, controversial topics apparently arose, and quick-tempered men let nature get the best of them for a few moments.

Again, the author wishes to stress that this story is not told for the purpose of taking sides or making one individual look better than another individual. The story is simply told for the purpose of amusing the reader and providing the reader with a bit of history regarding the path that led I.D. to his eventual destination.

At any rate, I.D. and some of the other members were no longer content in this church at the Frog Pond. It has been said that, at this point, basically anyone (regardless of denomination) who walked into the church and wanted to preach was permitted to get behind the pulpit. Also, church members were under the leadership of a moderator, who, according to some, was, in all probability, not an Old Regular Baptist. Unhappy with these conditions, some of the church members left the Old Indian Bottom Church at the Frog Pond.

This group of dissenters consisted of the following individuals: I.D. Back, Arch and Artie Cornett, Byrd Cornett (son of Arch and Artie Cornett), Blaine Cornett (uncle of Byrd Cornett), Jack and Irene Brown, Minerva Kimbley, Ann Collins, Coy Hampton (I.D.'s brother-in-law), and Gladys Hampton (I.D.'s sister).

On the Sunday morning following that controversial Saturday morning service, this group gathered for church services in a little schoolhouse. It was located at the end of a bridge that now leads to the residence of Elwood and Kathy Cornett. (Recently, this author visited with Irene Brown, the last living charter member of the Mount Olivet Old Regular Baptist Church, at the nursing home where she currently resides. On the bulletin board in her room, Irene has displayed a picture of this building. The caption below it reads as follows: "The Little Red School House." The reader will also find a copy of this picture in this book.)

Eventually, all of these dissenters took their membership to the Little Collie Church, which was in the Thornton Union Association. As Arch and Artie Cornett had actually been initially baptized by an Old Regular Baptist minister (Elder Watson Combs), they were taken into the Little Collie Church by recommendation. All other members of the dissenting group, however, had to be re-baptized so that they could be baptized into the Little Collie Church.

Over the years, there has been speculation by some Old Regular Baptist Church members, as well as by some members of other denominations, regarding why it is necessary, if indeed it is necessary, for someone from another church to be re-baptized before being accepted as a member into the Old Regular Baptist Church.

I have wondered about this issue myself. Hence, in a state of confusion, I posed this question to Elder Elwood Cornett. I felt that he, as moderator of the Indian Bottom Association, would be able to rationally explain the reasons behind this tradion. As is typical, he responded in a calm, educated, and reasonable manner. The sum of his response was basically that this is done as a means of reducing the possibility of conflicts among belief systems. In other words, if someone comes into the Old Regular Baptist Church from another denomination, it could arouse controversy if that new member tries to bring with him beliefs that were specific to members of the church to which he had previously belonged, and are not shared by members of the Old Regular Baptist Church. For example, if a person who had previously belonged to a Catholic church should decide that he or she would like to become a member of the Old Regular Baptist church, then that person is expected to leave behind those beliefs that are specific to those of the Catholic faith (e.g., confession of sins to a priest in order to obtain forgiveness) and take on the belief system of the Old Regular Baptists. In short, Elder Cornett contended that requiring someone to be re-baptized helps maintain "a clean line" among the churches via ensuring that the churches are not experiencing conflict and strife as the result of mixing together a lot of different denominational beliefs.

At any rate, I.D. Back, as well as most of the other members who came from the Frog Pond Church, was re-baptized. This second baptism was conducted somewhere in the Little Collie area by an Old Regular

Baptist minister named Ray Collins. In later years, when the subject of whether or not an individual moving from one church to another should be re-baptized, I.D. would lend his support to the belief simply by saying, "I did it."

Irene Brown recalls that she was baptized twice, and that I.D. baptized her on both occasions. On the first occasion, he and the moderator of the church at the Frog Pond baptized her together. The second baptism occurred on the day that Coy and Gladys Hampton were re-baptized. Irene remembers that, after seeing Gladys wade into the water to be baptized, she, too, waded into the river. At that point, I.D. Back and Ray Collins re-baptized her.

In time, the same members who had left the church at the Frog Pond would also leave the Little Collie Church. As was mentioned in a preceding paragraph, the Little Collie Church was in the Thornton Union Association. These individuals dissenting from this church decided to form a new church. They "got an arm" from the Little Collie Church, however, in that members of that church assisted them in setting up their new church. This is the group that would establish (in June of 1956), and become charter members of, the Mount Olivet Old Regular Baptist Church in Blackey. (While it was initially in the Thornton Union Association, this church entered the Indian Bottom Association in 1973.)

When asked if this was a difficult time for the charter members of the Mount Olivet Church, Irene Brown responded that it was not. "We enjoyed every minute of it," she said. "We worked together, laughed together, and cried together."

As was stated in an earlier chapter, the building that served as the church had originally been a theater. In time, however, the theater burned down. At that point, all that remained of the building was a foundation and a pile of debris. It switched owners several times over the course of the years. Eventually, the property was sold to the church members, and, using only the foundation that had belonged to the theater, they erected a building that would serve as their church.

There's a funny, fictional story (involving a talking parrot) that has been told among locals. As the story goes, this parrot (who had lived in the theater prior to the time that it burned) saw the church that was newly erected in the old theater's previous location. Reportedly, when the bird saw the first congregation assembling at the church, he recognized some of the faces as belonging to people who had also attended shows at the theater. Upon recognizing these faces, the bird reportedly squawked, "Same crowd! Same crowd!" The storyteller, upon mimicking the parrot, will then howl with laughter upon delivery of this punch line.

All teasing aside, however, this new structure (church) was very much unlike its previous structure (the theater). In contrast with the old building, which had featured films involving actors who entertained by acting out stories based on fiction, the new building was a location where reality was discussed. The speakers were preachers, who did not strive to entertain with stories of fantasy, but presented facts that would lead listeners to make the most important decision of their lives - to repent of their sins and be born again.

Left: The Little Red School House (Personal collection of Elwood Cornett)/Right: sign welcoming visitors to Mt. Olivet Old Regular Baptist Church today (Author's personal collection)

CHAPTER 16
Trying to Support a Growing Family

Shortly after I.D. became a preacher, he was blessed to become a father for the second time. This second baby was a daughter. On October 16, 1952, Sheridith Susan Back was born. The baby's middle name was given to her in honor of her maternal grandmother, Susan Hamilton. A beautiful, darkly-complected baby with dark tresses and dark eyes, she, like her older brother, bore a strong resemblance to Ina Rose.

Nearly six years later, I.D.'s third and youngest child would be born. On July 1, 1958, Ina Rose gave birth to Anthony Walton Back. This little baby with a broad forehead bore a stronger resemblance to his father than had his two older siblings.

The children's names would be shortened over the years. Ronald Wakefield would be called "Ronnie." Sheridith Susan would be called "Sherry" by friends and neighbors, although members of the immediate family would frequently refer to her simply as "Sis." Anthony Walton would come to be known as "Tony."

Throughout his children's lives, I.D. was a preacher. Raising children, however, requires money. Hence, in addition to his ministerial duties, I.D. also had to hold down a job that would provide him with money.

Well beyond the time of Sherry's birth, he continued working at Wardrup's Meat Packing Plant. When Ronnie was approximately 8-years-old, however, Wardrup's closed. At that point, I.D. was employed at a coal mine run by Harry Smith. He began hauling coal.

Around 1963, another job opportunity came along that would allow I.D., once again, to depart from the mining industry. His old friend "Byrd" Cornett engaged him in a business proposition.

A storeowner, "Byrd" had decided that he wanted to leave the "store keeping" business. So, he leased his store, which was located in downtown Blackey, to I.D.

I.D. had a history of "store keeping." His father "Little Jim" had, for a time, kept a store. At that time, I.D., of course, would have spent time alongside his father in the store. He had also spent time working in the store of Jack and Ann Cornett. Hence, he would take these past experiences with him, as he began the adventure of operating his own store.

Despite his past exposure to the store business, however, he had not learned enough to make his own business a success. Ronnie recalls that his father was very "soft-hearted." Hence, he would willingly sell a poor person groceries, regardless of whether or not that individual's credit rating was respectable. People soon learned of I.D.'s generosity, and some began to "take advantage" of him.

There was another store in town at the time. Ronnie remembers one occasion upon which he was standing with I.D. in front of the store and watching an elderly man, who owed I.D. money, going into the other store. Ronnie remembers his father saying, "Look. There he goes into Estill's store, and he still owes me on a bill that he ain't paid on in months."

A store will not stay in business if customers do not pay money for their purchases. Hence, within approximately two years, I.D. was finished with the "store keeping" business.

CHAPTER 17
Fatherhood

Ronnie, Tony and Sherry   Ronnie, Ina Rose, Sherry & Tony
(Personal Collection of Ronnie Back)

What kind of parents were I.D. and Ina Rose Back? There is evidence that they were not very different from other middle-class parents attempting to raise children in Southeastern Kentucky at that time. They both worked hard to ensure that their children would be fed and clothed. I.D.'s role was to work outside the home and earn money, while Ina Rose's role was to be a homemaker who supervised the children's daily activities and made sure that they were cared for properly.

Ronnie remembers feeling a special closeness to his father at a very young age. He stated, "Even as a little fellar, I realized that Daddy was a special person...a real good man." Ronnie further stated that, even as a young child, he had been able to understand certain things about his father that he simply could not express in words.

In fact, Ronnie remembers that part of the bond he felt with his father was forged by the ability to sense when all was not right in his father's world. For example, he recalls that once, shortly after his father became a preacher, there was concern about I.D.'s health. A growth had appeared in the upper part of his back, and doctors were afraid that he might be seriously ill. Young Ronnie did not understand the concept of diseases. He did recognize, however, that "there might be something bad wrong with Daddy."

In those days, few, if any, people had health insurance. People generally paid their own medical bills out-of-pocket. So, when I.D. was preparing to have this growth excised from his back, members of the church congregation donated the money (that was collected in the offering at the end of the Sunday church service) to help pay for his medical expenses. Ronnie, who, by this time, would have been approximately five-years-old, donated some change that he had been keeping in his pocket.

Ronnie also remembers that he often accompanied his father to church services and played next to his father, as the church service progressed. He didn't listen to the actual words of the preachers, as his young mind was likely occupied by a small car or some other toy that he'd brought along from home. He did, however, hear the cadence of the preaching, and, even as a young child, he recognized that preaching was a good thing. Specifically, he recognized that his father's preaching was a good thing.

Ronnie Back himself has been described by a former teacher as someone who, even at an early age, presented with an obvious goodness. Kind and gentle with others, his heart was easily touched (as remains the case today). This same teacher recalls being at a church service one day and observing a particularly moving exchange between Ronnie and his father.

I.D. was preaching a wonderful sermon, when suddenly he said something that triggered tremendous emotion in his young, tenderhearted son. At such point, Ronnie jumped from his seat, ran to the stand, and grabbed the legs of his preaching father. The teacher remembers that this was not characteristic behavior for any of the Back children, as both I.D. and Ina Rose made certain that the children were well-behaved (and drew no undue attention to themselves) during church services. This was not an act of misbehavior, however. This was simply an innocent child's response to spiritual emotions that were triggered by the message that God was sending from Heaven to earth via the child's father. The teacher has recalled that members of the congregation generally found this exchange to be very moving.

Ronnie is not the only child with fond memories of his father, however. Sherry also recalled some special times with her father.

One of her favorite memories of I.D. involves the knack that he had for imparting "funny little sayings" to his children. A favorite past time was to have the children memorize and recite their father's full name, which, according to him, was as follows: Isaac Dixon Woodrow Wilson Henry Nicodemus Samson Cicero Junior Back. Sherry did learn to recite this name from memory, but neither Ronnie nor Tony was able to do so. In years to come, the tradition would be carried on, and I.D. would also attempt to get his grandchildren to memorize and recite this lengthy name.

As the only daughter in the family, Sherry was doted upon by both parents. There is a special bond that often tends to exist between a father and daughter, however, and the bond between this father and daughter was no exception. In fact, I.D. doted upon his daughter so much that Ina Rose, per report of family friend Phyllis Asher, would sometimes say, "I declare, if I didn't know better, I'd swear that she was his favorite!" Of course, this was not the case, as I.D. loved his children equally. Still, that special bond that can only exist between a father and his daughter was present.

Despite being showered with love by her parents, however, Sherry would still suffer much at the hands of her brothers. Both Sherry and Ronnie recall that young Tony enjoyed fighting, simply for the sake of fighting. On one particular day, Tony had picked a fight with his older sister, and the two were arguing heatedly in the front yard of the Back house. I.D. warned them to stop, but the quarrel continued. So, he gave them another warning, but, still, the two continued their dispute. At this point, I.D.'s patience had reached its limit, and he promptly spanked both of the children. Sherry would later recall that it was the only spanking that she ever received at the hand of her father.

On another occasion, Tony went so far as to hit his sister on the head with the lid of a garbage can!

Not only did Tony pick fights with her and pound her head with a garbage can lid, but Ronnie also did his share to torment his younger sister. He often persuaded her to engage in role-playing activities that involved scenarios such as his being a jungle hunter and her being a lion, or his being a cowboy and her being an Indian. The end result was that Sherry the Lion or Sherry the Indian often got peppered with bbs from Ronnie's bb gun.

Ronnie remembers that, in those days, Sherry was a good sport who rarely tattled on her brother. If she happened to yell out in pain, however, and Ina Rose happened to hear her, then Ronnie would promptly receive a spanking at the hand of his mother.

Both Ronnie and Sherry recall that it was Ina Rose, not I.D., who was largely responsible for disciplining the children in the Back household. They remember that she was the parent who had to remain strict and render punishments, for I.D. was simply too tenderhearted to punish his children physically.

Ronnie would later remember one incident in which his father's inability to discipline the children was perfectly evident. On this particular occasion, Ronnie had been playing with a young neighbor. In the midst of their play, Ronnie had done something that he was not supposed to have done, and his comrade promptly ran to inform Ina Rose of the transgression. Before Ina Rose could come outside to address the matter, Ronnie climbed a tree in order to escape his mother's impending wrath.

When Ina Rose did come outside, she instructed Ronnie to come down from that tree immediately. Ronnie refused, and so she repeated the command. Again, Ronnie refused. This exchange continued for a while, with the result being that the more times Ronnie refused to come down from the tree, the madder his mother became. Eventually, she yelled up, "Ronnie Back! Don't you think I can't climb that tree and get you, because I can! I want you to get down from there right now!" Still, Ronnie refused to dismount the tree.

Alas, Ina Rose made a deal with her son. She told him that, if he would climb down from the tree at that moment, she would not, in Ronnie's words, "whip him too hard." Thinking that this was likely the best deal that he was going to get at this time, Ronnie slowly climbed down from the tree.

Unfortunately, his mother reneged on her part of the bargain. When he came down from that tree, she began to spank him, and she continued to spank him all the way into the house. He laughingly recalls that she would get to thinking about how he had acted about coming down from that tree, and then she would get mad and start "sworping" him again.

When I.D. came home from work that evening, Ina Rose was still fuming. She immediately told I.D. what Ronnie had done, and then she proceeded to tell him that he was going to have to go talk to him and "whip" him, because she simply could not have a child of hers being so disobedient.

Like many women (including myself), Ina Rose loved pretty shoes. Ronnie remembers that she had several pairs stacked on a shoe rack in the bedroom. When I.D. came into the bedroom to punish Ronnie, he instructed him to bend over that shoe rack. The plan was that, while Ronnie was leaned over the rack, his father would spank his little buttocks. Young Ronnie tearfully leaned over the rack and awaited his lashing. Alas, however, no blows fell upon him. When he turned around and looked with tear-filled eyes at his father, he realized that his father was also crying. At that point, I.D. returned to his wife in the kitchen and sighed, "Ina Rose, I can't lay a hand on that youngen'."

Ina Rose did not drive. I.D. worked through the week, and then he attended church services on the weekends. Also, during evenings and weekends, he was often called away from home for the purpose of performing ministerial duties (e.g., preaching funerals, performing wedding ceremonies). Because of these factors, and because Ina Rose was hesitant to let her children travel anywhere alone, lest they would not be watched as carefully as they would be watched when in her presence, the Back kids spent a great deal of time at home. Ronnie recalls that, prior to the time that he entered high school and could travel to ball games on the school bus, he had never witnessed a high school basketball game.

Once in high school, Ronnie remembers that he was "backward" and participated in no organized sports.

Sherry, on the other hand, did participate in high school sports. She was a cheerleader. Fortunately for her, she was able to ride to and from practice sessions and games via the school bus. At other times, she would catch rides with some of her friends. Had she not been able to travel via these alternative means, she would not have been able to participate in any extracurricular activities after school.

Not only did I.D.'s busy schedule prevent him from being able to transport his kids to a lot of school events, but, per Sherry's recollection, it also resulted in his being unable to be a spectator at many of these events. Nevertheless, she recalls that, when he was able to do so, he followed her to ball games and lent his support during the years that she served as a cheerleader.

She remembers one particularly funny story involving her father's eagerness to support his children in school activities. This particular story also involved this author's now-deceased aunt, Sondra Lynn Fields, who was on the cheerleading squad with Sherry. On this particular occasion, the cheerleaders were on the floor conducting cheers, when I.D. suddenly stood up from the bleachers and yelled, "Go, Sissy Bob!"

Sondra was someone who enjoyed joking with others. Hence, after witnessing I.D.'s cheer of encouragement for his daughter, she refused to let either him or Sherry forget about this incident. In the future, she would teasingly remind them repeatedly of I.D.'s outburst.

Ronnie remembers that, despite I.D.'s busy schedule, he always found time to take Ina Rose and the kids for a small vacation each year. He usually took them up into Ohio or down into the Smoky Mountains.

These vacations usually fell around the Fourth of July, as much of the business activity in those days revolved around the work schedule of coal miners. The one full week of vacation time that coal miners were given fell during the week of July 4th. Hence, that's when other companies often allowed their employees to vacation, also.

There was one particular trip that remained in the back of Ronnie's mind. During this trip, I.D. was driving the car, and Ina Rose was seated in the passenger seat. Baby Tony was in a car seat between the two of them. (The car seat, however, was not like modern car seats. One individual, remembering car seats as they appeared in that era, recalled that they looked more like the seats attached to today's baby swings.) In the back seat of the car, young Ronnie and Sherry were standing. Both kids were leaning forward against the front seat. Ronnie's tiny head was on one side of I.D.'s headrest, and Sherry's was on the other side. Hence, he was surrounded by children. As they stood, they continuously sang, as loudly as they could, "Knick, knack, patty wack, give your dog a bone." Meanwhile, young Tony, who could not yet talk, was imitating the sounds of automobiles, as he played with a toy steering wheel. Ronnie remembers that the noise finally made I.D. so nervous that he, in a good-natured manner, called out, "Knick, knack, knick, knack...is that all you two can sing?!"

Ronnie recalls another vacation during which I.D. and Ina Rose, trying to entertain the children and make sure that they enjoyed themselves, began engaging in play along with the kids. Ina Rose began the games when, at a playground, she climbed to the top of a slide and quickly slid to the bottom. Unfortunately, she landed hard on her buttocks, and, thus, was sore during the rest of the car ride. Upon arriving at the hotel, I.D. did his part to amuse the children. He climbed upon the diving board at the hotel pool and promptly dove into the water...only to land on his stomach! Thus, he, too, was sore for much of the trip. These incidents give evidence, however, of the lengths that this young couple would go to in an attempt to show their children a good time.

As the children grew into adulthood, there is evidence that I.D. continued to be more lax than his wife in the area of discipline. However, Ronnie recalls that, just as he had been able to sense in childhood when all was not right with his father, the father could now sense when all was not right in the world of the son. This made it especially difficult for Ronnie to hide his transgressions from I.D.

He recalls that there was one occasion upon which he, after having partaken of a few alcoholic drinks, was walking along the side of Highway 7. Much to his dismay, the family car soon pulled up beside him. I.D. and Ina Rose were going to visit "Mammy" (Ronnie's name for Callie), and they had stopped to see if Ronnie would like to ride along with them. The son was in a dilemma. He knew that if he declined the offer, he would immediately arouse suspicion. On the other hand, if he accepted the offer, his parents may well smell liquor on his breath when he climbed into the car.

Alas, with reluctance, he accepted the ride that his parents had offered him. Ronnie supposes that, in walking to the car, he must have staggered somewhat, because I.D. said to him, "What's wrong with you, Son? Have you been taking drinks?" Ronnie denied that he had been partaking of liquor, and he likely said little else, for, during much of the ride to his grandmother's house, he tried to hold his breath (lest I.D. or Ina Rose might smell the telling scent on his breath).

As soon as the family arrived at Callie's house, Ronnie remembers that he jumped out of the car and ran into the hills, where he promptly proceeded to regurgitate. Knowing that he was supposed to spend the night with his Uncle Walt, he did not come out of the hills, until such time that he was certain that his parents would have already left to go home.

Later that night, however, as Ronnie lay awake in bed, his conscience began to haunt him. The longer he stayed there and thought, the more it bothered him that he had lied to his father. He could not recall ever having told a bold-faced lie to his father prior to this instance. Finally, he could withstand the guilt no longer. Quietly, he climbed out of bed and got dressed. Then, he walked the distance (approximately one mile) from Walt's house to the home of I.D. and Ina Rose.

Ronnie entered the house and went to wake his father. Aroused from sleep, I.D. was a bit confused and mumbled, "Son, what's wrong?" At this time, Ronnie confessed to his father that he had lied earlier, and that he had, indeed, been drinking. Upon hearing his son's confession, I.D. responded, "I already knew that, Son. It just hurt me that you lied about it."

After relieving his conscience, Ronnie walked back to Walt's house, climbed back into bed, and was able to fall asleep.

On another occasion, Ronnie recalls that he and his father were doing some work around the house when he decided that he wanted to go buy a milk shake. A popular hangout for kids of that time was known simply as "Jean and Darrell's." Owned by Darrell and Jean Hampton, the restaurant sat at the bottom of School Hill. Letcher Elementary and High School sat atop School Hill. So, the restaurant got much of its business, during the school year, from students. The kids would walk off the hill during lunch break to sit in a booth and share lunchtime with their friends, or to sit on a stool by the long counter and sip a milk shake, while listening to tunes blaring from the big juke box near the door. Still others spent much of their lunch break playing with the pinball machines that rested against the back wall. During the summer months, however, school was not in session. Hence, a young man in need of a milk shake would have to drive, or be driven, to the restaurant. Knowing this, and knowing that he would really enjoy taking his father's 1966 Comet for a drive, made Ronnie's craving for a milk shake that much more powerful.

Initially, I.D. said, "Okay, Son. We'll take a break, and I'll drive you up there to get a milk shake." This was not the response that Ronnie had been hoping to hear.

"No, Dad," he protested. "There's no sense in you doing that. I can drive myself."

After a few minutes of discussion and listening to Ronnie's pleas, I.D. relented and told him that he could drive. He reminded him, however, that he was to go no farther than Jean and Darrell's Restaurant, and that he was to come home immediately after buying the milk shake. Ronnie agreed that, of course, this is what he would do.

Upon climbing into the car and beginning his drive up the road, however, Ronnie began considering how impressive if would be to his peers from school if they happened to see him driving around the community alone. He further thought about how he would be much more likely to be seen if he surpassed Jean and Darrell's Restaurant and drove an extra distance of approximately three miles (one way) to the nearby town of Isom. The more he thought about the advantages of driving himself to Isom, the greater the temptation to follow through on these thoughts became. Alas, he gave into this temptation. As he neared the Hamptons' restaurant, he kept his foot on the gas pedal, and he didn't remove his foot from the gas pedal until such point that he arrived in Isom.

Sure enough, upon arriving in Isom, Ronnie encountered some of his friends and acquaintances, and he got to experience the joy of knowing that these people had seen him driving alone. His mission had been accomplished. His joy was short-lived, however, for he knew that, if he did not return home soon, his father would find out that he had been disobedient. Thus, he reluctantly left his friends, and drove the car back down Highway 7, until he reached the restaurant and ordered his milk shake.

Then, to make up for lost time, he drove faster than he should have along the route from the restaurant to his home. Approximately one mile below the restaurant, he lost control of the car and went sailing over a hill. He landed in a creek that ran alongside the road.

Fortunately for him, he emerged from the car unscarred. A nearby resident who had witnessed the accident let him use a phone to call his father.

First, Ronnie had to inform his father that he was not hurt. Then, he had to tell him that he had wrecked the car and damaged it significantly.

Aunt Crittie, who lived near I.D. and Ina Rose, loaned I.D. her car. Per Ronnie's description, it was "a Plymouth with big fins." This is the car that I.D. drove to Carbon Glow to pick up Ronnie.

While awaiting his father's impending arrival, Ronnie was miserable. He knew that he had been disobedient to his father, and he knew that, because of his disobedience, he was going to be lectured and punished.

Upon arrival, I.D. inspected his son's body in an attempt to ensure that he had no injuries. Upon satisfying his mind that his son was unharmed, I.D. told Ronnie to climb into the car so that they could go home. Upon hearing his father's command, Ronnie began climbing behind the steering wheel of Aunt Crittie's Plymouth. I.D. stopped him by saying, "Oh, no, Son. You get in on the other side. You've drove enough for today!" That was all he said. There was no lecture. With that one quip, he was able to make his point without having to lecture the wayward child.

After the Comet, I.D. bought another car that was considered to be more prestigious. Ronnie recalls Ina Rose telling him, "Well, Son, your daddy's destroyed us. He's went out and paid $3,000 for a car! We'll never get it paid for!"

Later, Ronnie would also manage to damage this new car. While driving it, he hit a tree in the yard. Again, he was miserable. He trudged inside the house and admitted to his parents that he had damaged the car. He told them to get an estimate of how much money would be needed in order to get the car fixed, and he told them that he would pay for the repairs. "Yes, you sure will!" his mother angrily announced.

The cost of repairing the car was $200. Ronnie recalls going through the front door of his parents' house and giving the money to his father (in his mother's presence). As he left, I.D. followed him out the back door, which was located in the kitchen, and gave the $200 back to him. To Ronnie's knowledge, Ina Rose never found out about this.

Ronnie remembers, too, that, as he got older, he and his father were further bonded by a shared appreciation for the simple things in life. For example, something as simple as the feeling of water from the shower head beating against the body after a hard day's work was appreciated by both men. They also had a shared appreciation for nature, and would enjoy telling each other when one saw some special display of nature (e.g., a deer in the yard). Ronnie remembers seeing a wild animal, sometime after his father died, and, before remembering that his father had died, thinking to himself, "I'll have to tell Daddy about that."

CHAPTER 18
Vietnam

The 1960s was a turbulent decade. President John Fitzgerald Kennedy and his brother, Senator Robert Francis Kennedy, were both gunned down by assassins during this decade, as was civil rights leader Martin Luther King, Jr. There was also an ongoing controversy surrounding the Vietnam War.

Ever the patriotic person, I.D. Back wanted to assist his country in whatever way that he could. Being near forty-years-old, and in less than optimal physical condition (due to his age and to the injuries that he acquired during WWII), he knew that he would be of little benefit as a soldier. Instead, he wanted to use the talents with which God had provided him; thus, he wanted to offer his services as a chaplain in Vietnam.

In later years, Ronnie would recall that, upon hearing this news, Ina Rose "nearly smothered to death." The thought of her husband going to a far-away country, and being in the midst of exploding bombs and foreign soldiers carrying guns, sent her into an understandable panic.

Alas, however, her worries were in vain. The military refused to allow I.D. to serve in the capacity of a chaplain, as he had not completed the educational level to meet their requirements. This was fortunate for I.D.'s family. It was very unfortunate, however, for the soldiers fighting in war.

I.D. was such a talented counselor. He was blessed with an ability to relate to people, regardless of their age, socioeconomic status, or educational level. He was particularly talented in relating to young people. Neighbor Beulah Back recalls that he didn't condemn or criticize young people on occasions when they "did wrong." Instead, he attempted to find a way to draw them in closer to him and to the church.

One way in which he attracted young people to the church was this - always showing them kindness. I can testify to this personally. He always made me feel as if I mattered, and that he and the rest of the church members cared about me and wanted me to get saved, so that I could one day go live in Heaven.

When my boyfriend was diagnosed with Chronic Myologenous Leukemia in 1999, I heard from someone, although I no longer remember who that person was, that I.D. was hoping to get a chance to speak with both of us. Undoubtedly, he was going to use this situation to draw us in to the church. He was likely going to explain to us why it was more important now, than ever before, that we get God in our lives. Sadly, though, we waited too late. At the time that I.D. died, we had not yet visited him together.

Because of his talent in dealing with young people and counseling them, however, this author simply feels that it would have been such a blessing if those poor soldiers could have had him in their midst. As a former soldier himself, he could have offered them empathy. If a soldier began worrying about dying and going to Hell, I.D., as a called preacher of God's Word, could have testified to him in regard to what he needed to do in order to be saved. As for those soldiers who didn't have the good sense to worry where their souls would dwell for eternity if they should be killed in war, he could have preached sermons that would have undoubtedly called this matter to their attention and made them rethink it. (Upon learning that he was not allowed to serve as a chaplain and offer his services to these soldiers simply because he did not have enough formal education to meet requirements of the military, I recall saying, "Oh, my gosh! If they only knew what they were missing out on!" The military was being offered the services of one of the greatest and most-respected ministers in this country, and they refused him on the basis of a technicality.)

God knows best, however, and He has a Master Plan in which we all play a role. For some reason, that Plan did not include having I.D. serve as a chaplain in Vietnam. It called for him to stay in the mountains of Southeastern Kentucky and continue ministering to the people in that area.

In an interview, Ray Back echoed the sentiments of this author. He further stated, however, in regard to the topic of I.D.'s not being permitted to go to Vietnam, "I'm so glad that he didn't go, because we needed him so much around here!"

In reality, God made a way for I.D. to remain in the mountains (comforting and preaching to citizens therein) and still be of service to the soldiers in Vietnam. Audiotapes featuring some of I.D.'s sermons made their way to that foreign land so far away. Hence, he was able to preach to the soldiers via tape. Ronnie recalls that, when he attended college at Morehead State University, some of the male students there had spent time in Vietnam. Upon learning of his father's identity, they would say, "Hey! I heard tapes by him when I was in 'Nam!"

CHAPTER 19
Politics

After receiving the disappointing news that he would not be permitted to act as a chaplain to American soldiers serving in Vietnam, I.D. entered the political arena. As this was an era in which the Kennedy family was so highly respected, and as John Kennedy had opined that politics is one of the best fields through which an individual can serve others in the country, I.D. likely decided that he would help his country and its citizens via participating in local government and making changes on the home front (rather than traveling to Vietnam).

A cause-effect relationship is not being implied. There is no evidence that I.D. entered the political arena in response to being denied entry into Vietnam. What is being implied is this - I.D. was determined to serve God and his fellow human beings in whatever way he could. So, when one opportunity to offer service was denied by our country's military establishment, he simply looked for another way in which he could work to help others.

As politicians are often viewed unfavorably by many people, however, I.D. must have worried about the impact that his entrance into the political arena might have upon his image in the eyes of his fellow church members and in the eyes of those in the congregations to whom he was preaching. He certainly would not have wanted to do anything that would have lessened people's confidence in him as a minister, and, hence, lessened any influence that he might have had in leading them to the Lord.

At the time that he was debating a decision of whether or not to enter into the political arena, his store in Blackey was still open for business. Longtime friend Ray Back recalls going into the store one day and discussing I.D.'s concerns with him. He recalls that I.D. asked him, "Ray, What should I do?" In response to this question, Ray replied, "Well, I.D., if you want it [a political seat], all you gotta do is file. You won't have to campaign. You can just stay here and take care of your store."

I.D. did, indeed, file - and the race was on! He was running for county commissioner from district 3.

The first formal declaration of his candidacy, as far as this author could tell, ran in the February 25, 1965 edition of the local newspaper, *The Mountain Eagle*. There was simply a statement reading as follows: "*The Mountain Eagle* has been authorized to announce the candidates for local offices...." Under the office of District 3 Commissioner, the name "I.D. Back" was listed.

The neighborhood was abuzz with excitement about I.D.'s candidacy. As I.D. did have his store to care for, and as it might have seemed less than pious for a minister to engage in campaigning, friends and family members ran the campaign for him, just as Ray Back had predicted.

Ray recalls that his own stepbrother, Deward Brown, was responsible for campaigning in the McRoberts area of Letcher County. Various other individuals were responsible for campaigning in other areas of the county. Actually, as I.D. was already so well known and well liked throughout the county, little campaigning was necessary. Ray and Beulah Back opine that I.D. could probably have been elected to an office encompassing larger areas of Southeastern Kentucky, as his preaching of funerals in surrounding counties had resulted in his becoming basically as well-known and well-loved there as he was in his native county of Letcher.

Ray recalls the excitement surrounding the election. He remembers I.D.'s brother, Bill, saying, "Well, Ray, you reckon I.D.'ll make it?" To this question, Ray recalls responding, "Oh, yeah. He'll make it!"

And, indeed, he did make it. On May 27, 1965, I.D. Back won the Democratic primary for District 3 County Commissioner. Opponents listed in *The Mountain Eagle* were as follows: Harrison Boggs, Jr., Coy Wright, John Caudill, Lawrence Sumpter, Jr., and Bill Banks. When the votes were counted, it was determined that I.D. had received a total of 877 votes. According to the election results that were revealed in *The Mountain Eagle*, the opponent that came closest to defeating him in the election was Bill Banks, who had won 657 votes.

Shortly after the primary election, *The Mountain Eagle* ran an advertisement in which I.D. expressed his thanks to those who had supported him in the primary election, and he asked for their continued support in the upcoming general election (which was to be held on November 2, 1965). His statement, running in the June 10, 1965 edition of the newspaper, read as follows:

"I am humbly grateful to the good people of Letcher County for nominating me for County Commissioner, District #3. I shall forever *cherish* this vote of confidence from a wonderful people.

There are tremendous tasks ahead for the people of Letcher County in addition to the great projects already accomplished and under way. I pledge to you if elected your County Commissioner, to further every worthwhile project, whether it be sponsored by the County, State, or Federal government, or private effort for the betterment of the looks and the living of Letcher County people both Democrats and Republicans.

Let us now join hands for the great work we are planning."

In some issues of *The Mountain Eagle* published prior to the general election, the following campaign announcement was printed:

"To the Voters of Letcher County:
It is nearing the day of decision, the election November 2. This will be a very important election for the people of Letcher County. Great things for our people are under way and being planned. It is vital that we elect as Letcher County Commissioners men who understand and sympathize with these programs and who will see that they are carried out successfully. I have been active in learning what our people need and in helping plan these great programs.

If you will elect me as your County Commissioner for District 3, I pledge to you that I will do my utmost to see that everything possible is done for the betterment of Letcher County so that we and our children may have a better place in which to live.

The County Commissioner attends to the business affairs of the county. As a businessman, I pledge to you that I will carry out the duties of a Commissioner with complete honesty and justice to all.

I thank you in advance for your vote on November 2. - I.D. Back"

I.D.'s Republican opponent in the general election would be Howard Brown. After all votes were tallied on that November evening, it was revealed that I.D. Back had received 3714 votes, and Howard Brown had received 3129 votes. These results were reported in the November 4, 1965 edition of *The Mountain Eagle*.

He would run for re-election in 1969. As it stood, he was unopposed in that election. This author could find no listing of his name when results of the May 1969 Democratic primary election were printed in the newspaper. In regard to results of the November 4, 1969 general election, the November 6, 1969 edition of *The Mountain Eagle* revealed that, even though he was unopposed, I.D. Back had received 3400 votes. He would go on to serve another four-year term as County Commissioner for district 3.

Eventually, however, politics would, in the words of a family friend, "leave a sour taste in I.D.'s mouth." It has been alleged that some of I.D.'s fellow politicians had participated in some unseemly business, without his knowledge. When this unseemly conduct was reported by the newspapers, however, I.D. ended up, in the words of the same family friend, "looking bad" (even though he was reportedly innocent). Being a man of high moral character, he was deeply affected by the way that this political business had reflected upon him.

He had served for several years, and, per recollection of Beulah Back, fellow commissioners Deward Brown and Eddie Howard had nothing bad to say about I.D. in years to come. They, instead, would recall I.D. with fondness and with words of praise. Nevertheless, the negative experience that he had encountered during his political career was enough to make him leave the political arena permanently behind him. In 1973, he did not seek reelection.

A friend attempted to get I.D. to re-enter the field of politics in later years. As I.D. was, at the time, struggling somewhat financially, the friend thought that it would be a good idea if he sought election to the office of County Court Clerk. By doing this, he would have been able to earn some extra money for retirement. The friend told him that his kids could run the office, and he, thus, would not even have to deal with it. All he would have to do is get elected to the office (which would not have been a hard task for a man of his popularity). Then, while his kids were running the office and he was building up his retirement fund with the extra money earned via holding this political office, he would still have time to perform all of his ministerial duties.

The friend who made this suggestion, however, would later recall that I.D. was not interested in the idea. He wanted no part of politics anymore. In response to the suggestion that he reenter the political arena, I.D. reportedly said, "I've had enough politics already." He refused to seek the office of County Court Clerk.

CHAPTER 20
Doing "Church Work"

It was mentioned in a previous chapter that each association has a moderator. Within each association, each church also has a moderator. While he was never moderator of an association, I.D. did moderate several churches during the course of his lifetime. Among these churches were Mount Olivet Old Regular Baptist Church, Little Dove Old Regular Baptist Church, and Blair Branch Old Regular Baptist Church. (Additionally, he served as assistant moderator at some of the other churches.)

As a moderator, he was responsible for overseeing the "church work" (discussion of business issues relative to the church) at each of the churches that he moderated. It was his responsibility to ensure that appropriate procedures were followed, and that order was kept within the church, during the time that the "church work" was being conducted. It was also his responsibility to make decisions regarding which preachers he would ask to participate in the church services being held at those churches that he was moderating.

While it is true that he used a lot of humor in relating to people, it is also true that, when it came to doing "church work" and conducting church services, he was generally quite serious. Elder Ellis Adams, who served as assistant moderator of the Blair Branch Old Regular Baptist Church during the time that I.D. was that church's moderator, would testify to this in later years. Elder Ivan Amburgey, who acted as assistant moderator of the Little Dove Old Regular Baptist Church during many of the years that I.D. served as moderator of that church, would recall that I.D. would occasionally use humor himself, but that he kept a "tight rein" on the rest of the ministers and did not want them joking and laughing during the time that church business was being discussed.

Despite his efforts to remain somber (and keep other ministers somber) in church, the humor that naturally radiated from I.D. Back did sometimes manifest itself even as he stood in the pulpit.

For those unfamiliar with Old Regular Baptist church services, it is important that you be informed at this time that services typically last approximately one hour and forty-five minutes (not counting the 30 minutes of congregational singing that generally precedes the preaching). Members of the congregation do not listen to one preacher each and every Sunday. Instead, various preachers attend the service, and generally, at least four of them are asked to preach during the service. With so many preachers present to take part in the service, it is generally not well-accepted when one preacher takes more than his fair share of the time allotted for a church service.

As someone who has attended these church services since years preceding kindergarten, I have heard many preachers during the course of my lifetime, thus far. Too, I have heard many different sermons. Thus, there have been times that I experienced boredom, and became restless, during church services. This is wrong of me, but, unfortunately, it is true. This is particularly likely to happen when someone that we know as a "long-winded" preacher enters the pulpit.

This brings me to the discussion of a trait that I.D. Back and I had in common. For the most part, neither of us enjoyed listening for long periods of time to those "long-winded" preachers.

Hopefully, though, I was, and still am, able to conceal my annoyance and frustration with these preachers better than I.D. was able to conceal his feelings. After all, I had only my own boredom to worry about. He, on the other hand, had on his shoulders the responsibility of moderating these churches and ensuring, to the best of his ability, that the most effective preachers were put into the stand to preach to sinners in the congregation.

Elder Adams remembers that I.D. was primarily interested in making certain to "feed the flock." He was not interested in "playing politics," so to speak. Hence, he was not apt to ask someone to serve as one of the preachers at a church service simply because that person was one of his friends or acquaintances. He only invited into the pulpit those preachers who he thought could truly hold the crowd's attention and preach the Gospel to them. (In fact, Elder Adams has stated that one of the most important lessons that he learned from Moderator Back was the importance of using preachers with gifts.)

Because of his responsibility as a moderator and as a servant of God, he had little patience with those ministers who might be doing something to hinder the smooth flow of the church services, and, thereby, decrease the likelihood that a member of the congregation would hear something preached that would lead him or her to convert from sinner to Christian.

The mannerisms that he exhibited in the event that a preacher preached something that he did not agree with, or surpassed a comfortable time limit in the pulpit, became obvious and comical to those of us who would observe them time after time over the course of many years. Invariably, I.D. would begin shifting in his seat. Then, he would start crossing his legs alternately. Sometimes, he would raise his small hand to his mouth and begin gnawing his fingernails. After this, he would shift some more and begin sighing audibly. Occasionally, he could be heard to softly utter "Lord, Lord," while flipping through the pages of a songbook.

Then, he would push his glasses upon his nose. These actions were repeated, in no specific order, until such point that the offending minister ended his sermon and returned to his seat.

My own parents have laughingly recalled one incident that well demonstrates how bluntly I.D. sometimes chose to deal with the "long-winded" preachers. On this particular occasion, they were in attendance at a church service at which I.D. was also present. As the service progressed, one preacher chose to stand at the pulpit for quite some time. When the preacher finally sat down, I.D. rose from his seat and announced to those in the congregation, "Everybody, stand up and stretch."

Ronnie remembers another incident that gives evidence to I.D.'s impatience with preachers who stood too long in the stand. His father was attending a church service, and one of the preachers began preaching on the story about Jesus and the woman at the well. After a while, I.D. was ready for the preacher to take his seat, but the man continued to stand and preach. Another preacher in attendance, however, was enjoying the sermon and was in no hurry for the preaching to end. Hence, when the preacher who was preaching the sermon finally decided to end his sermon and sit down, the preacher who was enjoying the sermon encouraged him to continue by saying, "What about the woman at the well? You gonna leave her at the well?" Before the man could start preaching again, I.D. answered the other preacher's question by saying, "Yeah!"

I.D. was not trying to be hateful with the preacher in question. He was just, in a good-natured, humorous fashion, getting the point across to this individual that he needed to take his seat and let someone else preach for a while.

By making such remarks to preachers in a humorous manner, I.D. was able to convey his message, without angering fellow preachers and church members, much more easily than would someone who lacked his sense of humor and the level of popularity that he enjoyed in the church and in the community.

Ray and Beulah Back shared with this author another story that involved I.D.'s ability to make a point via the use of humor. He was going to a graveside service, and there were no other preachers there. Hence, rather than sing all songs alone, he asked one of the employees from the funeral home to assist him in singing. At this point, the funeral home employee, who shall remain nameless, agreed to help. As the man sang along with him, I.D. realized that he had made a terrible mistake in requesting this man's assistance, for he, apparently, was not a gifted singer. When the service ended and the two men were leaving the cemetery, I.D. turned to the man and said something to the effect of, "Well...I don't believe I'll be needing you anymore."

Indeed, he had a unique ability to make a point without angering others. It is good that he had this ability, because, per recollections of Elder Elwood Cornett and others, I.D. was someone who simply hated conflict.

If he thought that a conflict was about to arise, I.D. would become very nervous. He would fidget in his seat and exhibit some of those same mannerisms that he exhibited when a "long-winded" preacher was in the pulpit.

Elder Cornett recalls one situation in which I.D.'s distaste for controversy was evident. Not only is Elder Cornett moderator of the Indian Bottom Association, but also he, like I.D., used to moderate a few individual churches. Some of the church members from one of the churches that Elder Cornett moderated had become involved in a conflict. It seems that, allegedly, one church member had spread some false information about one of the church's ministers. The preacher about whom these false accusations had been made was a particularly high-tempered man, and he was not at all happy to be the subject of such vicious gossip. Even though the rumors were untrue, this gossip had done some damage to the preacher's reputation, and, he, undoubtedly, worried that these lies would lessen any influence that he might be able to have upon persuading sinners that they needed to be saved.

This was a situation that the moderator had to deal with, in order to help preserve the unity of the church. Rather than going alone on the trip to meet with the church members involved with this problem, Elder Cornett asked I.D., as well as Elder Fess Blair, to accompany him. He hoped that having them with him would help ease the tension. He also chose to have the offending church member go, in the presence of all three ministers, to the house of the offended preacher and offer apologies for the falsehoods that he had told about the man.

Elder Cornett recalls that, during the drive to the preacher's home, I.D., who knew this preacher well and, hence, was well aware that he tended to be
high-tempered and blunt, was extremely nervous about the matter. He was worried that controversy would arise in his presence. Alas, however, things went well, and the matter was successfully resolved. So, on the trip home, I.D. was much more relaxed. He even stated, "I feel a lot better leaving than going!"

Elder Ellis Adams says that he served as assistant moderator (to moderator I.D.) of the Blair Branch church from 1984 until the time of I.D.'s death. Hence, he can offer further testament to I.D.'s distaste for conflict. He recalls that sometimes, if I.D. thought that controversy was going to arise on the Saturday night when business matters were to be addressed, he simply would fail to attend the Saturday night service, thus leaving Elder Adams to deal with any conflicts at hand.

I questioned my parents about I.D.'s dislike for controversial situations. They recalled, also, that he truly did dislike dealing with such matters. They also recalled, however, that, when "backed into a corner," he would demonstrate the ability to deal with such matters effectively. Elder Adams agreed that I.D. could get angry just as easily as anyone else could.

Elder Adams recalls that I.D. Back "was not a hard moderator at all." Some people in the Old Regular Baptist churches have a tendency to want to pass laws within the association (applicable to church members) that are based largely on tradition, regardless of whether or not Biblical scriptures actually support these traditions. For example, some individuals in the church would prefer that female church members wear dresses (rather than pants) and never cut their hair. I have heard the scriptures used by people who support these beliefs, but I am not at all certain that they are interpreting these scriptures correctly. Perhaps they are right in these beliefs. Perhaps they are not. At any rate, the debate regarding such issues has, in times past, hurt the growth of the church (per I.D.'s own remembrance). Thus, he would not take time to address these issues. That is not to say that he did not agree with the teachings. He simply did not believe that these issues were important enough to argue over and risk bringing division to the church. He would, however, per recollection of Elder Adams, fight hard in support of those issues that did have Biblical scriptures supporting them.

My own father, perhaps, best described I.D.'s skill as a moderator. He simply stated that, "In moderating churches, I.D. used a lot of common sense."

Elder I.D. Back is pictured here with Old Regular Baptist minister, Clarence "Hawk" Dixon. (Photo from personal collection of Danny and Teresa Dixon.)

Pictured here is the Blair Branch Old Regular Baptist Church. Elder I.D. Back moderated this church for many years. (Author's personal collection)

CHAPTER 21
More of the Back Wit

While it is true that some of I.D.'s mannerisms were often noted and laughed at by members of the congregation, it is also true that he was not above laughing at himself. The late minister Clarence "Hawk" Dixon would sometimes recount a story about a time in which he and I.D. were conducting a funeral service together. Per Hawk's account of the story, I.D., seated on a stand in front of the congregation, crossed his legs and looked down at his foot, only to see that a black shoe was covering the foot. At that point, Hawk would recall I.D. saying, "I could have sworn I put on brown shoes!" It was at that moment that Hawk, amused, pointed to I.D.'s other foot and informed him that, indeed, he had put one brown shoe on his foot on that day, but that he had put it on the other foot! I.D. had mismatched his shoes! Upon taking note of this fact, the two men laughed in unison.

Another story that I.D. would recall and laugh about in later years centered around an incident that occurred when he was just a young preacher. According to my father's version of the story, I.D. and two other preachers (a young one and an older one) were standing on the bank of a river, waiting to take part in a baptism. As they stood there, the older minister preached. When he finished preaching, he proclaimed that the ministers should come down on their knees in prayer. Upon looking down and seeing the clay-like mud surrounding him, however, he determined that he really did not want to kneel in that mud. Hence, he turned to I.D. and the other young preacher and said, "One of you young bucks can hold prayer today!"

Indeed, few people in life could see humor in situations or could enjoy a good joke or prank more than I.D. did. Whether the person that he was talking to was old or young, and whether the person was a church member or not, I.D. would often try to make the individual to whom he was speaking laugh.

I can remember that, when I was a little girl, there were several times when I.D. called our house to talk to my father, and I answered the phone. There are people who would have simply said, "Can I speak to Danny?" without even acknowledging the person answering the phone, particularly when the person answering the phone is a child. I.D. Back was not one of these people, however. Before asking to speak with Dad, he would generally take a few moments to engage me in conversation. He would ask how I was doing, or something along those lines. Only then, would he say, "Is your daddy home, Honey?" When I would answer affirmatively, and ask if he would like to speak with him, I.D. would often jokingly reply, "Yes. Just tell him the governor wants to talk to him!"

My younger sister "Misti" (referred to as "Mit" by many family members and friends) is very close in age to I.D.'s granddaughter, Callie. When she was a child, she would go to Callie's house to play sometimes. Callie, her parents Doc and Sherry Back Fugate, and her half-brother Allen lived next door to I.D.'s house. Hence, Callie and Mit alternated between playing at Callie's house and playing in I.D.'s own yard. When he would look outside and see the two little girls engaged in play, he would playfully yell at Mit, "Get off my property, you Danny Dixon-looking thing!" He would then proceed to tell her, in a joking manner, that he did not want anybody related to Danny Dixon trespassing upon his land.

Just as I.D. played pranks on others, he sometimes had pranks played on him. He was a game victim, however, in that he would just laugh at the prankster's antics.

My father recalls that one Saturday night, upon leaving church services at Mount Olivet Old Regular Baptist Church and heading home, he and some other church members noted, upon passing I.D.'s house, that there was a fire burning near the home. A bolt of lightning had stricken a pole and ignited this fire, and there was danger that, if the fire proceeded to burn, it would eventually reach I.D.'s house and engulf it in flames. Ina Rose, who had been home alone (while I.D. was attending the church service at Blackey) was extremely scared, as anyone in her position would have been. So, my father and some of the other church members stopped at I.D.'s house and built a "backfire" to keep the fire from reaching I.D.'s home. Eventually, members of the fire department arrived and extinguished the fire, and everything worked out fine.

I.D. was not going to be allowed to forget this matter in an easy manner, however.

As was mentioned in a previous paragraph, there are different churches within the Indian Bottom Association, and, when someone joins the Indian Bottom Association, this new convert is asked to specify the name of the church to which he wishes to take his membership. My parents are members of the Cedar Grove Old Regular Baptist Church, as were several of the other individuals who had stopped to assist in controlling the fire near I.D.'s home. In contrast, I.D. and Ina Rose were members at Mount Olivet Church.

Cedar Grove's membership, at that time, had been increasing at a faster rate than had the membership of most other churches within the Indian Bottom Association. Hence, there was good-natured competition between Cedar Grove members and members of I.D.'s beloved Mount Olivet (referred to by many as simply "Blackey Church"). I can remember hearing my parents, during my childhood years, joke with Mt. Olivet members that a new "joiner" had come to Cedar Grove. The Mt. Olivet members would return the jibes when a new "joiner" took membership at their church.

Thus, as many of the "firefighters" were from Cedar Grove, and they had performed a service for a member of the Mount Olivet Church, it was decided that he should be "billed" for their services. My mother and father drafted a letter informing I.D. and Ina Rose that, as Cedar Grove members had endangered their lives fighting this fire at the home of a Mt. Olivet Member, a "bill" for these services (to be paid by those in membership at the Mt. Olivet Church) was being included in this correspondence. Then, they sent the letter, via certified mail, to Agnan "Ag" Back, the clerk at Mt. Olivet. (Mom and Dad did not sign their own names to this letter. They devised it to look as if it was an official letter coming from an entire group of people at Cedar Grove Church.)

The letter drew a lot of attention and amused many people, including I.D. Ag kept the letter for a long time after receiving it, and he would often pull it out and show it to people as a means of entertainment. One day, my father walked into the Cedar Grove Church (before services had begun), and the letter was being circulated among members of the congregation who had not yet had the opportunity to view it.

On another occasion, Mom went to a local post office, and, upon arriving at the post office, she saw Ag Back and James Dixon (who had once been quiet-natured, but who had become more verbal after joining the church) standing outside the post office. The two men were laughing and joking about the letter.

When telling the story of the fire, I.D. added his own twist to the plot. His version of the story was that "that Cedar Grove Bunch like to have burned my house down!" He told others in the community that, when he arrived home, the whole area was afire, and that the Cedar Grove members built another fire to ensure that his house did not escape destruction. His version of the story indicated that they had purposely attempted to burn his home.

The reader must remember that all of these things were done and said in fun. It was a matter that brought much joy and entertainment to a group of people, who were acting as if they were at battle, when, in truth, they were all very fond of each other.

CHAPTER 22
Being a Grandfather

I.D. Back became a grandfather for the first time in May of 1970, when Ronnie and Hester presented him with a grandson named Byron. In October of 1971, he became a grandfather again, when Hester Back gave birth to Jason "Ikey" Back.

While I.D. loved his two grandsons immensely, Ronnie and Hester recall that, when the boys were born, I.D. was still a very busy man. At that time, he was working, as well as performing ministerial duties, and he simply did not have a lot of time to spend with them.

In the early 1980's, Sherry Back married Allen "Doc" Fugate. At that time, I.D. became a grandfather, yet again, to Doc's young son, Allen.

On April 6, 1983, Sherry gave birth to a daughter. She named the baby Callie Susan, in honor of the mothers of both I.D. and Ina Rose. By this time, Byron was a teenager, and Ikey was on the brink of becoming a teenager. Allen, born in 1972, was not a young child, either. Hence, it had been a long time since a baby had been in the Back home. It had been an even longer period of time since a baby girl had been in the Back home. Therefore, both I.D. and Ina Rose treasured young Callie.

Hester Back recalls that Callie was a child who did not like to have her hair brushed. Perhaps she had a sensitive head, but, at any rate, she was very particular about who she would allow to touch her hair. Callie's mother suffers from arthritis, and, thus, there were days when she was simply unable to brush Callie's long tresses. On these days, it was I.D. who Callie allowed to brush her hair.

Each morning, before school began, she would go up to her grandfather's house and let him brush her hair.

Several years later, I.D. became a grandfather once more. This time, the baby was born unto Tony and Gina Back. Older now, and retired from work, I.D. had more time to spend with this baby. Entries from his journals indicate that he and Ina Rose simply doted upon this child. At times, they would baby-sit him. At other times, they would buy things for him (e.g., stroller). I.D. even wrote of visiting Anthony's school for a Grandparent's Day lunch.

Unfortunately, while I.D. and Ina Rose now had more time to spend with a grandchild, they did not enjoy the same level of health that they had enjoyed when the other grandchildren were young, and they simply were not able to do many of the things with Anthony that they would have undoubtedly enjoyed doing.

Soon after Anthony's birth, great-grandchildren began arriving. Shirley and Ikey Back presented I.D. and Ina Rose with their first great grandchild on July 28, 1995. This baby was named Sydney Blair Back. Two years later(December of 1997), Andrew Walker Back was born unto this couple. Meanwhile, Byron Back and his wife (Kristi) became the parents of a baby girl named Morgan. Later, Allen Fugate and his wife (Sue) became the parents of a baby boy named Ashton

By this time, I.D. and Ina Rose were not able to baby-sit the children. They did, however, enjoy their visits. I.D. spoke in journal entries of his great grandchildren's beauty. Ronnie has stated that, even when Ina Rose was near death herself, she spent much of her time worrying about baby Morgan, who was sick at that time.

A fifth great-grandchild, Allison Darryl, would arrive after both I.D. and Ina Rose died.

CHAPTER 23
John Preece

During the course of his life, I.D. Back made many friends. One man, in particular, however, became a source of support and friendship for him. This man's name was John Henry Preece.

Like I.D., John Preece was small in stature. Quite likely, he was several years older than I.D., but this cannot be stated with certainty, as John would never reveal his age. Even today, as his body rests in a grave in Knott County, the date of his birth is not listed on his tombstone. The most important characteristic that the two men shared, however, was this – each loved both God and the church.

Elder Ivan Amburgey would recall, in later years, that one night, after a Saturday night service at Little Dove Church, John exited the building and found a group of church members congregating around I.D.'s car and trying to "jump start" it. As I.D. missed a great deal of work (and, thus, lost many days' wages) so that he might attend funerals in which he had been asked to preach, he was not doing very well (financially speaking) at this time. John, in contrast, was a coal operator, who would seem to those around him to be doing quite well financially.

While the two were not well-acquainted at that time, Elder Amburgey recalls that John Preece approached I.D., as he stood by the car, and said, "I want you to come over to my office on Monday morning. I have a job for you."

On the following Monday, I.D. reported to the office, just as John had told him to do. There, he did, indeed, find that John had a job waiting for him. It was not just any job, however. It was a job that would perfectly meet the needs of a man who was trying to hold down a paying job and fulfill ministerial duties at the same time. This was a job for which I.D. would receive pay even on those days that he missed work for the purpose of attending a funeral, visiting the sick or mourning, etc.

Not only did John provide I.D. with a new job, but he also presented him with a new truck. He told him to use the vehicle as his family car.

In addition to giving I.D. a job and a new vehicle, John Preece helped provide I.D. with something that he needed a great deal of if he was to go about the area performing the work that God had in store for him to do. What did John provide for him? He provided time. Both Elder Ivan Amburgey and John Preece's widow, Wilma, recall that I.D.'s job involved his traveling to different locations to pick up different mining parts for John. While he was traveling along the way to pick up these parts, Elder Amburgey and Wilma Preece laughingly remember that I.D. would take time out to stop at the homes of acquaintances and join them for coffee and conversation. He was never rushed on his job, and Wilma recalls that John would just laugh whenever I.D. returned from his travels and spoke about having coffee with people along the route.

Elder Amburgey added a funny twist to this story. He stated that John Preece, as someone running a company, was often extremely busy. Hence, if he heard of someone being sick, and he was simply too busy on that day to pay the sick man or woman a visit in person, he would tell I.D. of the situation and release him from work time so that he could go visit with the sick individual. Elder Amburgey recalls that elderly women, upon being released from the hospital, would chide poor John and praise I.D. They would say to John, "Brother John, you never did come see me in the hospital. Brother I.D. came, though." Little did they know that I.D. was visiting them at John's request, or that I.D. was

135

"on the clock" with John's company even while he was visiting with them!

John also, over the years, developed an understanding of I.D.'s problems. He, like most other people who were well-acquainted with I.D., knew that he became easily upset when faced with situations involving conflict. In regard to church conflicts, there were few places where such conflict was more likely to arise than at the annual gathering (of members from all of the Indian Bottom Association's different churches) at the Indian Bottom Association Building.

Knowing of how very upset I.D. would sometimes become as a result of events happening during this gathering time, John left a key to his house hidden in a special place. Hence, if I.D. ever needed to get away from the Indian Bottom Association Building or another church where a conflict was presented, he was able to come to John's house (regardless of whether or not anyone else was in the house) and relax there.

Wilma recalls one incident in which she was offended by a woman who had spoken hatefully to her one day. Very sensitive herself, Wilma returned home crying, only to find I.D., sitting in one of her living room chairs and ringing his hands because of an issue that had faced him, and upset him, at the Indian Bottom Association Building. The two commiserated for a while. Then, they both felt better and laughed about the fact that they had become so easily upset by the hurtful actions of others.

In years to come, as the two men and their families became closer, I.D.'s job description expanded. No longer was he just to go on trips to pick up equipment parts and then deliver those parts back to the office. Now, he and Ina Rose also got to take trips to John's farm in Nicholasville, Kentucky (just outside of

Lexington). On the farm, I.D. performed chores that John needed him to do.

The farm, however, was not just a place for I.D. to work. It was also a place where he and Ina Rose could visit (and escape from some of the pressures of home for a while), yet still be close enough to home that I.D. could return quickly in the event that he was needed to perform one of his church duties.

One of I.D.'s favorite past times was fishing. On the farm, John had several ponds that he kept well-stocked with fish. He also had his own ATVs (all-terrain vehicles), such as four-wheelers and motorcycles. While these vehicles were a source of great entertainment for the two aging gentlemen, they were also a source of danger.

One day on the farm, I.D., who was likely in his sixties at the time, was riding around on the motorbike. He turned his head for a moment, so that he could check to ensure that the path to his right was clear. As he did this, however, he accidentally veered to the left and collided with one of John's neatly-planted trees.

Elder Ivan Amburgey recalls that, a few nights later, at a Saturday-night church service, I.D. arrived in poor condition. He had sustained some broken bones during this motorbike accident, and, thus, he was too sore to attempt to preach. Elder Amburgey recalls I.D. commenting to the congregation that he was not able to do much that night. At that point, John jokingly pointed out that he would be able to do a lot more if he had not run into that tree!

Alas, however, John's teasing would come back to haunt him. Sometime after I.D.'s accident, John found himself to be the victim of a similar accident. Elder Amburgey would recall that five, large dogs from a neighboring farm had been venturing onto John's farm and chasing his cattle. Hence, one day on the farm, John climbed onto one of his four-wheelers and rode out into the pasture so that he might scare away the offending dogs. While engaged in herding, John's eyes met the eyes of one of the dogs, and, for a moment, locked. During that brief instant, the four-wheeler veered in another direction, and John ran directly into a fence. He was knocked from the four-wheeler to the ground. Resting there on the ground, trying to catch his breath, he spent several minutes trying to determine whether or not he was dying!

These are not the only amusing incidents that would occur during the years in which I.D. and John befriended each other. In one interview, Wilma Preece would recall a particularly funny incident. She remembered that, during one visit to the farm, John had gone out to one of the stores in Lexington and purchased an absolutely beautiful suit for himself. Several days later, I.D. visited the farm, and, on this occasion, John took him to one of the stores in Lexington and bought him a beautiful suit, also. John did not recall the details in the design of the suit that he had bought earlier for himself; hence, he was not aware that the suit that he was purchasing for I.D. was identical to the one that he had already purchased for himself. This was soon to be brought to his attention, though.

On the following weekend, the two gentlemen walked into the Little Dove Church...looking very dapper, indeed, in their dark blue suits. The only difference in the attire of the two was a slight deviation between the ties that they were wearing.

Wilma recalls that John was extremely embarrassed. She also recalls that he knew that I.D. would be feeling embarrassment, too, because he knew that I.D. was sensitive to the fact that some people were already making remarks such as the following: "John and I.D....where you see one, you'll see the other!" Still, there was nothing that either of the two men could do about the situation at this time, except to just "get through" the church service and call as little attention as possible to their attire.

When John arrived home from church, however, he did take action to make sure that such an embarrassing incident never again occurred. He told Wilma to find someone who would be able to wear his blue suit and give it to that person. So, she remembers that she gave the suit to a minister named Bill Moore.

A few nights after this incident occurred, I.D. and Ina Rose came to John and Wilma's home for a visit. At some point during the evening, Wilma remembers that John turned to I.D. and said, "Well, Ike, go ahead and wear your new suit wherever you want to. I took care of the problem. Wilma gave my suit to Bill Moore."

At that point, per Wilma's recollection, I.D. and Ina Rose exchanged quick, horrified glances. Then, I.D. turned to John and said, "Brother John! You don't mean it! Surely you didn't!" After John assured him that, indeed, he had given his suit to Bill Moore, I.D. exclaimed, "I gave mine to Brother Agnan Back!"

Now, neither of the two men had one of the beautiful blue suits to wear!

Over the course of the years, a beautiful friendship would ensue between these two men and their families. Sherry Back Fugate recalls that the two became as close as natural brothers. John and Wilma and I.D. and Ina Rose vacationed together, attended church together, and visited together. How could they not become close? Wilma recalls that there was one wintry day when the electricity at the Back home went down for a time. Poor

Ina Rose was ill when this happened, and John and Wilma invited the Backs to come stay with them until such time that the electricity was restored.

Elder Ivan Amburgey would recall in later years that, during the years that John and I.D. were friends, no one could say anything negative about I.D. in John's presence, and nobody could say anything negative about John in I.D.'s presence, and get away with it. Wilma further attested to this fact with a story that she told about John. She recalls that one of John's employees once made a negative comment about I.D. in John's presence. The comment centered around the fact that I.D. was able to miss days of work and still receive pay for the days that he had missed. Wilma remembers that John became irritated upon hearing this comment, and that he quickly informed the offending man that he was never to say anything negative about a man doing God's work to the extent that I.D. Back was doing. John told the man that, in his opinion, they all had a duty to do whatever they could to assist I.D. in being able to do the work that God had for him to do.

In hindsight, it seems that John did exactly that...whatever he could do to enable I.D. to do the work of God without hassle.

After many happy years together, however, I.D. was saddened to learn that his longtime friend had been diagnosed with lung cancer. In later years, Wilma would recall that John sustained a bump on his chest during the 4-wheeler accident that he was involved with on the farm. She would wonder time and again if that accident could have ignited John's cancer. At any rate, whether caused by the accident or not, a serious illness was attacking John's body.

Throughout the sickness, I.D. provided moral support. Even though his beloved Ina Rose was also ill, I.D.

would sometimes leave her side for a while so that he might sit by the bedside of this man who had been such an important fixture in his life and in the life of his family. Wilma recalls that I.D. was with John on the day that he died. She remembers him looking up at her from the foot of John's bed and saying, "It won't be long now, Wilma."

When John died of lung cancer in 1999, I.D., along with my family, myself, and many other people who had come to know and love John Preece, was truly saddened. In a journal entry recorded on that day, I.D. spoke of John's death and described him as simply "a good man." What an accurate description that was!

CHAPTER 24
Preaching and Singing

What kind of preacher was I.D. Back? Why was it that so many people esteemed him so highly and that so many people gave their lives to God after listening to him preach? In response to these questions, Elder Ellis Adams said with a smile, "I wish I knew!"

First and foremost, I.D. submitted himself unto God. He was willing to do whatever it was that God wanted him to do. In return, God rewarded him with a great gift...the gift of delivering sermons in such a manner as to lead sinners unto repentance.

This is true of many preachers, however, and, still, not all are adored the way that I.D. was adored by both Christians and sinners.

I can still recall him standing behind the pulpit on so many occasions, when the "lot had fallen on him" to preach. (When "the lot has fallen," this simply means that the majority of preachers in attendance at a service are urging one particular preacher to be the next to offer a sermon. When this occurs, it is generally agreed that this is a sign that God wants this particular preacher to enter the pulpit and preach the next sermon.) So many times, before he began his sermons, he would begin singing in a soft, soothing voice,

"As I stand at the banks of the river,
Looking out over life's troubled sea,
I see an old ship a'sailing.
Is that the old ship of Zion I see?"

Gradually, the volume would increase, but the voice would remain soothing, as he crooned on.

"Her hull was beaten and battered,

From the storms of life, I could see.
The waves were high, but the old ship was sturdy.
Is that the old ship of Zion I see?"

By the time that he sang the next stanza of the song, his voice would likely be filled with emotion. Still, he would sing on.

> "At the stern of the ship was the Captain.
> I could hear, as He called out my name.
> 'Get on board, for this old ship is leaving.
>   It will never pass this way again.'"

Generally, members of the congregation would have joined along in the singing of this hymn at the beginning of the second verse. By the time that he began singing the fourth verse of the song, it would not be at all unlikely to hear shouts of joy from the congregation, as they raised their arms in the air and shouted praises to God. Still, I.D. would continue singing.

> "When I step on board, I'll be leaving,
> All my troubles and heartaches behind.
> I'll be safe with Jesus, the Captain,
> Sailing out on the old ship of Zion."

By this point, when the song was concluded, it was not uncommon for I.D. to be so overcome with emotion that he would immediately launch into a spirit-filled deliverance of the Gospel. At other times, he would spend those first few moments, following the song's conclusion, simply talking to the congregation. Then, gradually, he would be overcome by the Spirit of God, and the true preaching would begin.

He often used natural matters in an analogous manner so that people could better understand what he was trying to say to them. For example, the above song (which, according to Ronnie Back, was a favorite of grandson

Ikey) is not really about someone sailing on a ship. Instead, it is about a person who is dying and making the journey from earth into Heaven. Still, by comparing this journey to one made on a ship that carries us away from a world of trouble and woe and into the paradise of Heaven, I.D. was able to simplify his message so that even an uneducated person would be able to understand what he was saying.

Not only did he use analogies in songs that he sang, but he also used analogies during the preaching of sermons and the deliverance of advice. For example, if he told someone to "get the gears on," he was telling that person that he needed to get to work. He used these words, because, having grown up on a farm, he knew that a horse or mule was ready to work as soon someone put the gears on it. So, when word came to him that a family friend was seeking God, I.D. sent word that this person needed to "get the gears on." He was saying that the person needed to get serious about acquiring salvation and start praying fervently to God for forgiveness of his sins.

Another factor that was helpful in making I.D. such an effective preacher was this - he was often personally acquainted with most of the members of a congregation. These people saw him out in the community throughout the week and knew how he lived his daily life. Hence, they knew that he was sincere in what he was saying in his sermons and that he actually did, as the old adage proclaims, "practice what he preached." He was not asking them to do anything that he had not done himself, and he was advising them what to do so that they might escape the fires of Hell. People appreciated this.

They were not being lectured by someone speaking to them via a television set - someone who would probably never meet them face-to-face or call them by name. They were not being lectured by someone whose daily life they could not observe for themselves, so that they might know if the person lecturing them was, indeed, living the type of life himself that he was advising them to live. Instead, they were being counseled by their friend and neighbor, I.D. Back, who was kind to them any time that he saw them in public, despite the sinful lives that they might have been leading. They were being counseled by a man who had comforted them and/or their families in times of mourning and visited them in times of sickness. They were being counseled by someone who truly had their best interests at heart and, who, according to their daily observances of him, truly was a man of God.

Also, I.D. was not above reaching out to people by leaving the stand and walking out into the congregation, while continuing deliverance of his sermon, so that he might urge people individually to call upon God and be saved. He would ask them, "Don't you want to join the church?" My own father can attest to this. He recalls that, in August of 1976, at the Cedar Grove Old Regular Baptist Church, I.D. came back into the congregation and saw him crying. At that point, he approached my father and said, "Honey, don't you want to join the church?" In response, Dad replied, "Yes! I sure do!"

Over the course of the years, some people would offer criticism of I.D.'s tendency to walk out among members of the congregation as he delivered sermons. Thus, he did this less frequently in latter years. Elder Ellis Adams believes that this was a mistake, because, just as I.D.'s question had assisted my father in taking that initial step in joining the church, he had done the same for many others. As he knew almost everyone in the community and could call them by name when he spoke to them, Elder Adams believed that this truly did make a difference in convincing people who had been saved to go ahead and join the church.

Much of the criticism received came from those who said that, when I.D. entered the crowd while preaching, he was begging people to join the church. This is not what he was doing. He did not want someone who had not yet been saved to go ahead and join the church anyway. He wanted such people to first obtain God's forgiveness of their sins and then join the church. Going out among the members of the crowd was simply his way of offering moral support to someone who had already been saved and really wanted to join the church, but was simply timid and ambivalent about the prospect of walking to the front of the building, in front of many people, and declaring an intent to become a church member. It was an attempt to let people know that he truly did care about the welfare of their souls and that, if they were living in their sins, they needed to pray that God would forgive them. It was not an attempt to beg sinners to join the church prior to obtaining salvation, however.

Both Ronnie and Sherry recall, too, that their father never tried to be something that he wasn't. With I.D. Back, what you saw is what you got, and he expected other people to be themselves, as well.

Ronnie recalls that I.D. was once called to preach in the funeral of an employee at Morehead State University. Ronnie accompanied his father to the funeral, but stepped outside a few minutes before his father had finished preaching his sermon. As the service ended, Ronnie recalls that two gentlemen exited the building together. Not knowing that I.D.'s son was standing nearby, one turned to the other and commented, "I never considered myself a high-hatter!" It seems that I.D. had preached about how the deceased man had not gotten "above his raising" and, despite his success in life, remained true to himself. Ronnie said that, apparently, this statement had "hit home" with these gentlemen and had "scorched them pretty bad."

Not only did I.D. Back not esteem himself above others, but he also felt discomfort if anyone else tried to bestow upon him undue reverence. Ronnie recalls one occasion upon which I.D. and Walt traveled to a church located outside the state. Upon seeing I.D. enter the church, the church moderator chose to stand up and recognize him in front of the entire congregation. Allegedly, the man talked at length about I.D. being a great preacher and their church members being so privileged to have him in attendance. I.D. apparently felt it was inappropriate for this man to bestow such praise on a mere man such as himself, when the time could have been spent praising and worshiping God. He reportedly became so upset that he left the stand and went back to sit among members of the congregation. He refused to return to the stand with the other preachers on that day.

I.D. Back at a baptism
(Personal Collection of Elwood Cornett)

CHAPTER 25
Offering Comfort And Fulfilling Duties in Uncomfortable Situations

While friends and neighbors may have once doubted the genuine nature of I.D.'s salvation and said among themselves that he would not last thirty days in the church, he did much in his life as a Christian that proved these people wrong. Not only did he preach sermons and moderate churches, he also, as has been frequently mentioned prior to this point in the book, had other duties as a preacher (e.g., preaching funerals, performing wedding ceremonies, visiting sick and mourning).

My father's parents were not Old Regular Baptists. They were members of a Pentecostal church, and Dad and his brothers were raised up in that religion. Still, I recall that I.D. Back, feeble even then, managed to attend the funeral of my paternal grandfather in 1999.

My mother's family members, however, are largely of the Old Regular Baptist faith. Hence, they have relied even more upon I.D. during times of distress.

Mom's family, during the 34 years that I have been alive, has experienced its share of death. In 1975, my mother's sister drowned in Lexington, Kentucky, as the result of a freak sailing accident. In 1982, my maternal grandfather died unexpectedly, when he suffered a heart attack at the relatively young age of 55-years-old. In 1988, my maternal great-grandmother, who lived with my grandmother at the time, died. In 1996, my mother's brother was killed in a car wreck.

In 1975, I was only three-years-old; hence, I can now recall only sketchy details regarding my aunt's death. While I cannot picture I.D.'s face in those sketchy memories, I know in my heart that he must have been in my grandparents' home, at some point, during the days that they suffered through the initial horror of this tragedy. I know this for two reasons. First, I have heard other family members mention I.D.'s presence when they discussed events surrounding the mourning of Sondra's death. Second, I.D. was acquainted with both of my grandparents, and, in times of sorrow, I.D. was virtually ALWAYS there for friends and neighbors in need of comfort.

For the other family members' deaths, I recall him being there for my family and me. There is a large picture-frame window in my grandmother's living room. Through that window, those sitting in her living room can see people opening the front gate and walking up the driveway that leads to her front yard. Whenever a family member has died in the past, friends and family members have congregated in that living room and mourned together. There is a particular chair (a recliner) that my grandmother has been seated in during these times. That is where she has sat and shed tears. That is where she has sat when accepting visitors arriving to offer words of condolence.

I remember sitting in that living room with Granny (or, at other times, out on the porch with other family members) during times of mourning and seeing I.D. come trudging up the driveway. Upon entering the house (or upon stepping onto the porch, if there happened to be any family members sitting there), he would hug members of the family and say, "God bless you, Honey. I'm sooooooooooooo sorry!" I remember one time, in particular, when he was consoling Granny. He made mention of the fact that poor Granny had sat in that chair so many times and mourned the loss of so many loved ones. He understood that Granny had experienced a significant amount of loss and pain during the course of her lifetime, and he knew that she always sat in that particular chair during times of mourning, because he had been there for all of us through each of our mourning periods.

That was another special gift that I.D. had been blessed with. Even in the bleakest of times, he could offer comfort. He really did not even have to say anything. Just knowing that he was in our midst brought comfort.

It was not just church members and their families that I.D. comforted. He considered people throughout the country, particularly those in Southeastern Kentucky, to be his friends; hence, when trouble visited their homes, he could be counted on to come there and offer help. In fact, he did not even stop with family and friends. He would go to offer comfort and preach funerals anytime that his services were requested, even when he did not know the person or people who were making such requests of him.

To this day, I.D.'s name is frequently mentioned during the course of church services. I recently heard Elder Jim Fields (father of I.D.'s granddaughter-in-law, Shirley Fields Back, and maternal grandfather of 3 of I.D.'s great-grandchildren - Sidney, Andrew, and Allison Back) preach a sermon, and, during his preaching, he made some reference to I.D. He recalled hearing I.D. say once, upon learning of the death of someone who he did not even know, "Oh! I must go to that family!"

Ronnie recalls one occasion when I.D. was called to preach the funeral of a deceased member of a motorcycle gang. Ronnie worried about this, because he supposed that, when one of these gang members died, the death was likely commemorated via parties conducted in a wake-like fashion. He felt certain that there would be drinking and cursing, and possibly even fighting, and, hence, he was concerned for his father's safety. So, Ronnie warned I.D. not to go to this funeral.

He remembers saying to his father, "Now, Daddy, them fellars ain't like you and me. They're hard people." I.D. responded to his son's warning by saying that, be that as it may, they had called him to preach this funeral, and, therefore, he was going to go preach it.

Ronnie says that he worried the entire time that his father was gone to the funeral service. That evening, however, I.D. returned to his home unharmed. When Ronnie called to check on him, he learned that members of a motorcycle gang aren't necessarily as hard-hearted as he had believed them to be. His father told him of a big, burly man, dressed in black leather and chains, who had approached him after the funeral service. I.D. had been a bit unnerved when he saw this man coming toward him, for he did not know what the man had in mind. As the man ambled closer, however, I.D. had noticed that he had tears in his eyes. He patted I.D. on the shoulder and said, "Buddy, you sure know how to get to a fellar, don't you?"

Ronnie says that, after this incident, he never worried much about his father going to different environments for the purpose of doing the Lord's work.

Sherry and Ronnie both recall that their father would talk to anyone. Sherry says that the main thing her father taught her in life was that, no matter what someone else had done, she should still be kind to that person and not treat him/her rudely. I.D. taught his children this lesson, not just through words, but also through example.

In fact, this is one characteristic that people interviewed by this author have consistently noted in their discussions about I.D. Back. He did not discriminate in regard to who he would engage in conversation. He would sit down and talk with a sinner just as eagerly as he would sit down and talk to a Christian. Actually, he may have been even more eager to engage sinners in conversation, because he knew that talking to them would provide him with an opportunity to tell them about God and attempt to convince them that they needed to repent of their sins and be saved.

During the 1960s and 1970s, a local dining place known as "Christine's" was popular among those in the Blackey, Red Star, and Ulvah communities. Located approximately four miles below Blackey, near the Red Star Curve, Christine's was a small restaurant, whose employees specialized in home-cooked meals. Locals of all ages gathered here regularly. The cook, Christine Dixon Eldridge, was famous in the lower part of the county for her roast beef sandwiches and delicious hamburgers.

On one particular occasion, a group of men was gathered around a table at Christine's. One of the men was the uncle of Hester Back, Ronnie's wife. They had been drinking and were nearly, if not completely, intoxicated, when none other than I.D. Back walked through the door of the restaurant. Never one to shun sinners, I.D. walked directly to the men's table and began conversing with them. One of the men would later recall to Ronnie Back that, upon seeing I.D. come through the door, he thought, "Oh, my gosh! There comes I.D. Back!"

The men were embarrassed for a well-respected preacher such as I.D. to see them in their current state, but they knew that it would be considered ill-mannered if they didn't ask him to sit with them at their table. They felt certain that he would refuse their invitation, however. So, one of the men said, "Well, I.D., you're welcome to join us, if you don't care to correspond with those who've been partaking from the bottle." At that point, I.D. jerked a chair from under the table and immediately sat upon it. As he did this, he cheerfully proclaimed, "Why, sure! You're the very ones I need to talk to!" The man that extended the invitation had been so sure that I.D. would decline his offer that, upon hearing the preacher's response, he later told Ronnie that he was so stunned that, at that moment, he "could have fallen through the floor!"

Not only was I.D. undeterred in his pastoral duties by the questionable character of a person in need or the fact that he was not acquainted with a person requesting his help, but he was also, on occasion, undeterred by weather conditions. In April of 1987, an unexpected snowfall, approximately thirty-six inches deep, blanketed the mountains of Southeastern Kentucky. Weather conditions were so treacherous that even United Parcel Service (UPS), by whom my father is employed, was closed. (This fact is proof that the weather conditions were horrendous, because UPS rarely closes for any reason.) The roads were too slick for us to travel on, and, hence, my parents, my sister, and I were entertaining ourselves by riding a sled down a steep portion of Highway Seven that runs by my parents' home.

Things were relatively peaceful for a while, as there was not much traffic on the road. Soon, however, we heard the unmistakable hum of a nearing engine. Rick Whitaker was coming down the road in his four-wheel drive vehicle. Riding in the passenger seat of Rick's vehicle was none other than I.D. Back. Rick was taking him to participate in a funeral service at Brashear's Funeral Home.

I.D. had known that he was called in this funeral service, but he did not have a four-wheel-drive vehicle in which to travel. So, he had bundled up in warm clothes and begun walking down Highway Seven in an attempt to reach the funeral home, which is located approximately fifteen miles from his home. He had hoped that someone would come by and offer him a ride, but, if they did not do so, he was prepared to make the entire trip via foot. As it happened, though, God once again took care of His faithful servant and let Rick happen by in his vehicle, which was well-equipped for travel in treacherous weather conditions, and offer I.D. a ride.

Recently, Rick recalled this incident himself. He recalls that, upon arriving at the funeral home, he asked I.D. if he would like for him to wait until the funeral ended so that he could drive him back home. I.D. responded that that would not be necessary, as he would be able to catch a ride home with another preacher who was also in attendance at this particular funeral.

CHAPTER 26
A Preacher's Wife

I recently heard an elderly friend say that, if a minister is to be successful, he must have a good wife supporting him, because, if that is not the case, then his wife can hinder his success as a minister. There is truth in this statement. I.D. Back had such a supportive wife in Ina Rose.

While I.D.'s children were home and he was away attending to ministerial duties, it was largely left to Ina Rose to see that the children were cared for and brought up correctly.

Not only was she often left alone to raise her children, but she also spent many lonely hours herself. This author feels quite certain that Ina Rose, being much like other women, would have enjoyed spending more time alone with her husband. She would probably have enjoyed having him home to eat dinner with her and the children and discuss the problems of the day on many of the nights that he was away preaching funerals. She would likely have enjoyed spending a Saturday shopping for new clothes for her family and herself, or just getting out and taking a ride around the community, instead of staying on the home front, while her husband was off performing yet another ministerial duty.

Ina Rose, however, was, during many of the years that she was married to I.D., a Christian herself. As a Christian, she understood that it was vitally important that I.D. do what he thought the Lord wanted him to do. She understood that God had duties for him to fulfill, and that it was necessary for her and the children, as well as I.D. himself, to make any sacrifices necessary to ensure that he performed these duties well.

While Ina Rose accepted the fact that her husband was out about the Lord's business (as he should have been) and made the sacrifices necessary to provide her support, I, as a preacher's daughter, am guessing that her outlook regarding certain aspects of life was likely altered by these circumstances. For example, this author has heard that Ina Rose received criticism from people who claimed that she did not like for I.D. to have a lot of company when he was at home. I do not know if she truly felt this way, but, if one puts herself in this woman's shoes for a moment, it is entirely understandable why she might have felt this way. After all, between the time that he spent doing the Lord's work and the time that he spent trying to earn money to support his family, I.D. was left with very little time to spend alone with his wife and kids. On those rare moments that they did have together, it would have been extremely intrusive to have someone outside the family come into their home and rob them of that time together.

Also, as one never knows when someone is going to die and a preacher is going to be called in the funeral, it is very difficult for preachers and their families, at times, to plan ahead for vacations, etc. One preacher recalls hearing Ina Rose say that she and her husband were once passing through Whitesburg, on their way to some vacation destination. As they drove through Whitesburg, I.D. looked at the marquis in front of the funeral home and saw the name of someone that he had known. Knowing that he would probably be called to preach in the funeral, they ended the vacation before it even began and went back home.

Elder Ivan Amburgey would recall that I.D., even if he was not called in the funeral service, did not like to leave the area when a friend or acquaintance was deceased. He would simply say to Ina Rose, "No, I can't go. He was my friend. I need to stay here for the funeral."

This is not to say that ministers and their families are not honored when a family requests that minister's presence at an event. He is doing God's work, and is honored to do so. The family, in turn, generally feels honored that someone would have enough confidence in this family member to request his presence. That last statement is based on experience, as I know how honored I feel when someone asks Dad to preside over a special occasion in their lives, and I would guess that I.D.'s family felt much the same way.

Still, preachers and their families are human. Like other humans, these people look forward to spending time together, taking vacations together, etc.; hence, when a ministerial duty results in long-awaited events being cancelled, we, despite being honored, cannot help but feel the same level of disappointment that anyone else would feel in the same situation. That's just nature.

These statements are simply made so that the reader gets a better understanding of why it was that Ina Rose Back might have sometimes felt a bit resentful when people intruded upon the rare private moments that she was able to share with her husband and kids.

Readers must keep in mind that, had it not been for Ina Rose Back, we the public would not have had nearly as much access to I.D. Back. After all, had she not been willing to stay home and look after his children and make sure that they were fed and bathed and put to bed on time, he would have needed to stay home and do these things. If he was staying home and doing these things, he could not have been out preaching sermons, conducting marriage ceremonies, conducting funeral services, visiting the sick and mourning, etc.

Hence, we should be grateful to Ina Rose and her children for their willingness to share I.D. with us all for so many years. Both she and her children should be esteemed for the personal sacrifices that they made as a result of sharing him. They should not be condemned for any resentment that they might have felt toward individuals who intruded upon those few moments that they could share with him alone.

While not everyone has considered Ina Rose's contributions to I.D.'s ministry, however, she was not unappreciated by him.

Later in life, as was mentioned earlier, I.D. began recording daily journal entries. Generally, these entries were short, and they tended to reflect upon things that were important in I.D.'s life at the time of the writing. Entries centered mostly around the following topics: performance of the Lord's work (via preaching funerals, attending church services, visiting the sick, performing baptisms, conducting marriage ceremonies), friends and members of the community, his kids and their families, and his wife.

While Ina Rose was mentioned throughout the journals that I.D. kept over the course of the years, her name became a more common sight in entries made when both she and I.D. were ill. While he obviously felt poorly himself, he placed more focus upon Ina Rose's health. It was as if it brought him comfort just to be able to write something about his wife.

I commented to Ronnie and Hester Back about the fact that, no matter what the overall subject matter of an entry was, I.D. would refer to Ina Rose in some way. He might have written, for example, "The weather is good today." He would not stop writing at that point, though. He would generally add some comment such as "Ina Rose had a good day today" or "Ina Rose is sick today." It's as if she was always in his thoughts. Upon hearing me say this, Ronnie and Hester laughed and nodded in agreement. "She was," Hester stated, "his life."

Ina Rose Back suffered poor health for many years. She had undergone heart surgery. She was very frail in appearance. Regardless of how ill she had been in the past, however, she had always seemed to recuperate in time. As the years progressed, though, she began to experience longer, more frequent bouts of poor health.

By the spring of 2000, word was spreading through the community that Ina Rose would probably not be with us much longer. There were times, at this point, when I.D. was unable to attend church services, because Ina Rose was too ill to be left home alone. There were other times when he, undoubtedly with a broken heart, left his ailing wife in the care of one of their children, while he went and fulfilled one of his ministerial duties.

By the end of April 2000, her health had deteriorated badly. One night during that time, she reached a point when it was unlikely that she would see the light of another Southeastern Kentucky morning.

I remember the night of Ina Rose's death, because I remember my mother telling me, when I called home on that night, that a member of the Back family had called and asked that Dad come to Ina Rose's side as soon as he possibly could, for they feared that she was dying.

Hester Back would tell me in later years that Ina Rose was very fond of my father and would often take comfort in his words. She stated that Ina Rose could be feeling really poorly on a given day, but that, if Dad happened to stop by for a visit, she would, after he left her side, tell the family members that she was going to be alright, because Danny Dixon had said that she would.

On this night, however, Dad was unable to get to Ina Rose in time to tell her that she would be "okay," in the natural sense of the word. As a UPS driver, he often works long hours. Thus, it was quite late by the time that he was able to arrive at the Backs' home, and, by the time he did arrive, Ina Rose had already left this world.

With her at the time of her death, according to daughter Sherry, were the following individuals: her beloved I.D., Ronnie Back, Doc and Sherry Back Fugate, Ikey and Shirley Fields Back, Sydney Back, Callie Fugate, and Elder Jim Fields. Sherry would later recall that Elder Fields had said a nice prayer for Ina Rose shortly before she died.

Recently, I asked my father what he remembered about the night of Ina Rose Back's death. He said that one of the things that he most remembered was that, after Ina Rose had died and the family was discussing funeral arrangements, I.D. had wanted to keep the body up for approximately half of a week, so that the funeral might be held on a Saturday, when more people would be able to attend. Alas, however, his kids dissuaded him on this issue by reminding him that such arrangements would be in the best interest of neither the family nor the community.

Hence, Ina Rose's funeral service was held on a weekday. Despite the fact that the family had opted not to postpone her funeral until the weekend, a great crowd still filed into the Mount Olivet Old Regular Baptist Church on the day of her funeral.

I.D. and Ina Rose Back (Ronnie Back's personal collection)

CHAPTER 27
Life After Ina Rose

After the death of his beloved Ina Rose, I.D.'s health deteriorated rapidly. His children would recall that he had been ill prior to her death. At the time of her death, however, he lost one of his main reasons for living.

Still, following Ina Rose's death, he did experience a few happy moments. One of the happiest moments came when he was reunited with his old army buddy, Bernie Reed.

In 2000, one of Bernie Reed's family members happened to type in the name "Ike Back" on the Internet. He had, no doubt, heard the name many times over the course of the years, and he was curious to know if he would be able to locate the name via the worldwide web. When he typed in the name, a website, with a phone number, appeared. He called the number and learned that he had reached the residence of I.D.'s grandson, Ikey.

A reunion was scheduled. Bernie was brought to Blackey. Many people from the community attended this special event at the Blackey Senior Citizens Center. Family members and members of the Mount Olivet Old Regular Baptist Church prepared food for I.D., Bernie, and all others who were in attendance at this special reunion.

Ronnie and Hester recall that I.D. was so happy after the reunion took place. As frail as his health was at this time, he, miraculously, did not even become overly fatigued by the reunion and the excitement that came with it.

In the time following Ina Rose's death, regardless of how ill I.D. became, he maintained a sense of humor.

Following Ina Rose's death, a church member named Cull Collins sometimes stayed with I.D., and helped take care of him. On one occasion, my father went to visit I.D., and, on that occasion, Cull mentioned to I.D. that he would bring him a rabbit to eat if he wanted it. (Cull enjoys rabbit hunting in his spare time.) At this point, I.D. said that he would like to have a rabbit to eat, but he wondered aloud who would prepare the meal. Cull informed him that either he or his mother would be glad to prepare the rabbit for eating. At this point, with a twinkle in his eye, I.D. remarked, "Let your Mammy cook it, Honey!" He, apparently, was uncertain about Cull's culinary skills.

CHAPTER 28
I.D.'s Death

Hester Back thinks that the "beginning of the end" of I.D.'s life came on the day that he underwent a lung biopsy. She recalls being told by the doctor, on that day, that he might live a few days or a few months.

Sherry Back Fugate thinks that things took a turn for the worse when I.D. fell. As was mentioned earlier, he had tried to get out of his hospital bed and had taken a fall that left him with several injuries. At that point, he was hospitalized, and then he was placed in the Letcher Manor Nursing Home (where he stayed only two days prior to his death).

During an interview with Elder Elwood Cornett, I asked him if he recalled the setting of I.D.'s death. He responded that he did have that recollection.

Upon arriving at I.D.'s bedside, Elder Cornett was alone with him for a period of time. Later, one of I.D.'s children (Elder Cornett no longer recalls if it was Sherry or Ronnie.) stopped in to check on I.D. Upon finding him in a worsened physical condition, the child who had stopped in immediately called and alerted the other child. Soon, both Ronnie and Sherry were at I.D.'s bedside. A few others were also present in the room, as the time of I.D.'s death drew near.

The tiny room in which I.D. rested was faintly lit by some dim lights shining above his hospital bed. As Elder Cornett recalled, the lighting was neither too dark nor too bright. I.D. was sleeping, but his sleep was not peaceful, as he was having difficulty getting a breath of air. Still, considering the fact that he was dying, he was not struggling a great deal. Alas, he took a final gasp for air.

Elder Cornett recalls that I.D. had a peaceful, "easy death." With that final gasp for air, he slipped peacefully into eternal paradise to rest forevermore in the arms of his Savior, Jesus Christ.

CHAPTER 29
The Journal Entries

In previous chapters, the author sometimes referred to I.D.'s journal entries. It is true that he did write entries in journals throughout many years of his life. The earliest entries that this author could locate had been written in 1979, and the entries continued up through 2000 (just prior to the time of I.D.'s death).

In 1979, I.D. would have been 54-years-old. At the time that the last entries were recorded in 2000, he was almost 75-years-old. Between 1979 and 2000, the world in general underwent many changes. The themes of I.D.'s journal entries, however, remained largely consistent. Sometimes, work was mentioned. Duties and events related to the church, as well as the names of church members, were referred to a great deal. Family members, friends, and neighbors were frequently mentioned. Occasionally, reference would be made to the fact that a particular day was the anniversary of some event that had occurred during World War II.

With the exception of a few entries in which he had recorded some of his most profound thoughts, the entries tended, in fact, to be a bit monotonous at times. Some may even seem meaningless to the reader. The themes remained consistent, however, because the entries reflected what was important in I.D.'s life. Furthermore, what was important in his life did not change over the course of the two decades from which his entries were taken. Thus, there was not a lot of room for deviation in the topics of his journal entries, and the topics that he wrote about were definitely not meaningless to him.

Ronnie remembers his father as being someone who loved God above all else. His other loves included his country, his family, and his friends. Per Ronnie's own words, his loves ranked "pretty much in this order." The journal entries give evidence of this. (Regarding his love for his country, one can only imagine how troubled he would be about the turmoil that rages in today's land. He once said, during an interview, that the only hope for our country is that we return to the morals upon which it was, through blood,sweat, and tears, originally founded.)

Many of the entries were hurriedly scrawled, and, thus, the author was sometimes unable to read some of the words that he had written. When referring to names that she was unable to decode, the author generally put the initial of either the first or last name (depending upon which part of the name could not be decoded). Occasionally, grammatical errors will be corrected by the author; however, I.D. wrote as he spoke. As he made a habit of just being himself, he did not try to hide his Southeastern Kentucky dialect and the "grammatical errors," as those who speak Standard American English might refer to them, which are part of this dialect. Thus, the reader who is not used to this dialect may think that grammatical errors are present. Just remember that they are appropriate for a person speaking this dialect. Also, with a few exceptions, the author did not correct spelling, capitalization, or punctuation errors. The entries are typed largely in the same manner in which they were written.

Because these entries provide further evidence of the fact that he led his life largely by giving to others, despite the fact that personal sacrifices were required, the author is including some of the entries in this chapter. Hopefully, by reading the entries that are included in this chapter, the reader will be able to gain an even greater understanding of the sacrifices that I.D. Back made for the purpose of helping his fellow human beings and performing the work of God.

As I.D. aged, and his health deteriorated, journal entries became noticeably shorter. Earlier journal entries, which were written in the prime of I.D.'s life, however, tended to be longer and more profound.

An initial entry, recorded in 1979, reads as follows:
"When Jesus ascended back into Heaven, there were two men in white apparel. They told all of the men..., 'Why stand ye gazing into Heaven? The same Jesus that you see going shalt come again in like manner.'"

Following this entry were a few recordings relative to which of I.D.'s acquaintances had died in recent days. There were also, in some cases, comments regarding the condition or event that attributed to the demise of each of these individuals. There was also an entry in which I.D. had written the following heading: "Need to go see before Christmas." Under that heading, he had listed the names of 14 different individuals.

His entry on July 9, 1980 read as follows:
"What has happened to our church? (Watch and pray.) Have we let the world take the joy away from us? It seems our churches do not have the Great Spirit in it that we use to have. Have we gone from serving the Creator to the creation? God is not worshiped with things made by hand. He is a Spirit, and he seeks such that do worship Him in spirit and truth. The inner man is so hungry. Yet the outer man seems to want more attention (?)." (The question mark at the end of this sentence indicates that the author thought, but was not certain, that the last word written was "attention.")

"Christ Jesus the Lord, came and suffered all the worst things, and was not received of His own. When He came to them, a man of sorrow and agony with grief, He said He was the Light of the world, and when He went away, He said now we are the light of the world, so we are commanded to let our lights to shine. Surely we can do that for Him, after all He did for us. Let us put on the armour of light and cast off the words of darkness."

On July 18, 1980, the following entry was recorded:
"How much do we love our church and what we stand for? Do we love the world more than our church? When we who served in the army, navy, marines, and air force, we were committed and took an oath to uphold and defend our country. Well, to me, when we came to the church, after we had been <u>saved</u>, we also said publicly that we believe in our Lord and would defend His teaching, ordinance, and precept (?)." (Again, the question mark indicates the author's uncertainty as to whether or not the last word was actually "precept.")

"Why do some want to rebel and do as the world and say it don't matter? Yes, it does matter. You are a stumbling block to others. It is wrong to lose interest in your church. Christ said, 'Take up the cross and follow me.' That means I'm right."

Additional entries are recorded below (and on pages following this one).

March 14, 1981: "Ina Rose sick. Went to funeral of John Adams's daughter."

March 15, 1981: "Little Dove Church. Funeral for M.. Ina Rose still sick."

April 6, 1981: "Worked hard. Went to Funeral Home. Service for H. Stamper."

July 13, 1981: "Worked. John and I flew to Louisville to see S. Caudill. He told us that he was at peace with God. John Preece is a good man. Also seen J.M. Combs." (John Preece owned a private plane, and he would sometimes use it to fly himself, as well as other preachers and their families, to perform ministerial duties in places that were not close to home.)

Aug. 1, 1981: "Went to Hazard. Had wedding. Judy and Dannie Campbell. Church at Blackey."

Aug. 13, 1981: "Worked hard. Drove truck. Also went to Hazard Hospital and Nursing Home to see sick. Jenny still fair." (This last comment is made in reference to Ina Rose's sister, Jenny. I.D. had referred to her illness in some of the entries that preceded this one.)

Sept. 8, 1981: "Worked. Called about Brother Wesley. Not much better. Sister Bertha Combs in hospital at Hazard. Bro. Ova Hampton much better of surgery."

Nov. 2, 1981: "Visited the sick all day and went to B. Funeral Home for service for Fields lady."

Nov. 3, 1981: "Voted for Brother Manis Ison. Went to see E. Frazier." (Manis Ison, minister and former moderator of the Indian Bottom Association, had decided to seek the office of magistrate. Despite the vote of confidence from his longtime-friend, I.D., Elder Ison was defeated in the election.)

Nov. 26, 1981: "All of our family - Ronnie and Hester, Byron and Ike, Tony and Sherry, Ma and Pa - for Thanksgiving. Also, funeral service for B. Halcomb."

Dec. 31, 1981: "Worked. Went to Virginia Hospital and went to church - old year out and New Year in."

Jan. 19, 1986: "I went to Blair Branch Church. Then, I went to a funeral for C. Whitaker - Elwood and I. I went to see Aunt Maggie at the hospital. Tony had to go work."

Jan. 20, 1986: "I went to work today. Then, I went to see Walton. A 3-inch snow. Then I went to see Hattie Stewart. Then, Critty (Stewart) and I went to see his sister, A. Stewart. I went with brother S. Watts to the Br. Funeral Home. Services for R. Watts."

March 14, 1986: "I took Walton to the doctor. He is much better today. I went to Watts funeral. I tried to rest some at home. I also went to Hindman Funeral Home services for Jim B., of Knott County."

March 15, 1986: "Ina Rose and I went to Hazard. I went to the hospital to see the sick (Bro. Wilson C., and others). Came home and I went to Whitesburg Hospital to see Bill C., and others (A. Combs, O.Day, C. Halcomb, and others). I went to Blair Branch Church and we gave Gillis and Robert and Brad the right hand of fellowship." (In this last sentence, I.D. is likely referring to Robert Holcomb, Brad Breeding, and Gillis Reedy.)

March 29, 1986: "I went to see Walton first of all and then I went to Little Dove for the funeral of Sister Oma Asher. Come back to the Bull Creek Church and married a young couple - Scott Dixon and Barbara Jent. Then, Ina Rose and I went to Whitesburg. I went to the hospital to see the sick."

May 13, 1986: " I went to see about Walton and went on to work. John and I went to Whitesburg for the funeral of JD Collins. Come home sick. I also went to visit C. Cornett and Mose and Tab Stewart."

July 4, 1986: "I am 61-years-old today. I went up to see Vina and brought Aunt Crittie home. The kids come to see me on my birthday. I went to Knott funeral service for R.B. Adams."

July 18, 1986: " I went to work today. On my way, I stopped to see Walton. He was very well. I went to Hazard and also to L and S at Floyd County. Come home and went to sleep. Took a good nap and then went to Blair Branch Church for the baking of the bread for Communion."

Sept. 5, 1986: "It was the first day for our association. Vote for moderator and officer. A great introductory sermon by Brother Danny Dixon. Brother Elwood Cornett, Brother C., and I had the funeral of Donald Adams. Went back to the Association Building. Brother H.A. preached a great sermon. I took Ina Rose over to Brother John's and Hester with all the friends." (During September, Indian Bottom Association members meet for several days. During these days at the Association building, business matters are discussed downstairs, food is prepared and brought into the dining room, and church services are held upstairs. It is a busy and important time of the year. Generally, church members just refer to this time of the year as "the Association" or "Association time." That it what I.D. is referring to in the first sentence of this journal entry.)

Sept. 11, 1986: "I went out to work for half of day and came home and went to Letcher Funeral Home and had service for Homer Campbell. Went back to the funeral home services for Doris W. Back."

Oct. 16, 1986: "Worked on John's farm. Come home and went to Letcher Funeral Home - services for Aunt Vina Dixon. Today is Sherry's birthday - 34. Ina Rose and I went to have cake and ice cream with her."

Dec. 16, 1986: "Ina Rose and I went to see our doctors today and went on to Hazard and I went to the hospital to see Sister L.M. and V.S."

(Author's Note: There were two separate articles found in the 1986-87 journal that were of great interest to this author.

One of the articles found was half of a picture that I had, in times past, often seen in its entirety. The picture was of my father, and it was part of a picture that had been taken of my parents and me when I was approximately six-years-old. Upon finding this, I immediately took the picture and showed it to my mother. At that point, I wondered aloud what had happened to the rest of the picture. It was then that my mother informed me that she remembered how I.D. had come to own that picture.

She stated that, one day, she and my father had stopped at Squire Watts's store, and, within the store, some people were having a birthday celebration for I.D. (Squire Watts, who owned the store at that time, is also an Old Regular Baptist minister.) As a joke, Dad took from his wallet a copy of the picture featuring all three of us, cut himself out of the picture, and presented that cut-out picture of himself as a birthday gift to I.D.

While this incident was not commented upon in the journal, the picture did rest between pages marked for the month of July, and July was, of course, the month in which I.D. celebrated his birthday. He had kept that picture for all of the years passing between that July day in 1986 and the time of his death in 2001.

Another article that brought interest, as well as sadness, to this author was a page from a calendar. The date was January 15, 1987, and, on the front of this calendar page, I.D. had written the words, "We lost Walton today." On the back of the page, he had written these words, "My brother died on this date 1987. A real sad and lonely day."

That touched my heart so much, because, as someone who is very close to my own sister, I can just imagine how hurtful the loss of a close sibling would be. I had known before reading this that the brothers were close, and that I.D. had been immensely saddened by Walt's death. In reading his words, however, I was allowed to have a personal glimpse into just how truly sad he was, and I was just overcome by sadness for this man who had lost his brother.)

Dec. 10, 1989: "Tony was in a bad wreck."

Dec. 10, 1989: "God spared my son from death, also five others. I do hope...he will take heed and turn from sin to God."

(The author can also elaborate on the two entries listed for December 10. I remember that night that Tony wrecked. I remember that my sister and I were staying all night with my grandmother, as our parents had gone to Lexington -probably for the purpose of Christmas shopping. At any rate, I was resting on Granny's couch, trying to fall asleep, when I heard a siren go by the house.

My mother, in remembering this event, says that she and Dad had just returned from Lexington and stepped through the door of their house, when they saw the ambulance pass. Dad, at that point, said, "Something's happened." So, he and my mother climbed back into their car and followed the ambulance, so that they could find out what had happened.

Upon finding out that the ambulance was traveling to the site of a car accident, Dad, as a minister, did what he could to help. He went down to the site of the accident and talked to the victims. At that point, he found out that one of the victims was I.D.'s son, Tony.

So, Dad and Mom went home, and Dad called I.D. It was approximately midnight, but he was not in the bed. He, too, had heard the ambulance go down the road earlier, and he was waiting by the phone, in case Tony had, indeed, been involved in an accident.

Dad said to I.D., so as not to make him panic, "He's alright. I'll be up to get you in a minute." At that point, Dad went to drive him to the hospital to be with Tony.)

"The Day of Lord 1990: O Lord, support us all this day long until the shadows lengthen and the evening comes, and the busy world is hushed, and the fever of life is over, and our work is done. Then, in Thy Mercy, grant us a safe lodging and holy best and peace at last; Through Jesus Christ our Lord. Amen."

On the following page, there were notes reading as follows: "Hosp. Lexington, Jimmie White - V.A. Hospital, Linda Combs - U.K. Med. Center." (These were likely written as reminders to himself that, when he went to Lexington, these were the people that he needed to visit.)

(Occasionally, I.D.'s journals were difficult to follow, because he had a tendency to jot his thoughts from one year into a journal of a different year. Plus, in addition to daily entries, he would jot miscellaneous notes, such as the one referred to above. One note in his 1990 journal read as follows: "World War II veterans gone on." Then, he listed the following names: "Walt Back, Wayne Back, Byrd Cornett, Emil Cornett, Vance Cornett, L. Dixon, Mack Whitaker, Ike Whitaker, C. Whitaker, Jr. Hogg, E. Hogg." Another note read as follows: "Prayer for these. John Whitaker, Roy Cornett, and Nannie Back..")

Jan. 3, 1991: "We kept Callie today. She was sick. I went to Hurricane Gap Church service for E. Huff."

Jan. 5, 1991: "I kept Callie ½ the day. I went to see Brother Bob Gilley and Austin Miller who is sick. I went to Brashears' Funeral Home serv., for Flora Fields."

Jan. 12, 1991: "Brother Victor Campbell came and fixed my water pump for me today. I also went to the hospital to see Austin Miller and others."

Jan. 14, 1991: "Ma died 24 years ago today. Ina Rose and myself went to Hazard and ate out and got groceries. I felt bad."

Jan. 15, 1991: "I went to see the sick today at their homes and hosp. I feel a lot better."

Jan. 16, 1991: "We went to war today against (Aroch?)." (Again, the question mark is indicative of the author's uncertainty as to which word I.D. was intending to write.) "We pray for a quick ending."

Jan. 22, 1991: "2 years ago today Bill died. I went to Brashear Funeral Home for Homer Callahan's funeral. Also, Ina Rose and I went to the hospital to see Jina, Tony's wife."

Jan. 27, 1991: "I went to Cedar Grove Church. Danny Campbell and Irvin Ison joined the church. Brother Elwood and I baptized Randy Campbell. I also went to Lott's Creek Church...a good meeting."

Feb. 1, 1991: I went to Dr. Adams this morning and then I went to Hindman for the funeral of Delmas H. Brother Bob Gilley died today. Brother John and I went ... for Brother Banner Mann's services."

Feb. 3, 1991: "Our church time at Blackey. Brother Lane Campbell joined the church. Brother Agnan and I baptized Bro. Danny Campbell. Also met at Blair Branch Church for special prayer service for our men and women in the war. A great time."

Feb. 4, 1991: "I went to the hosp., and nursing home, to visit the sick and shut in. Also, I went to see Thelma Cole. I took Ina Rose to Hazard and ate out. I went to see John Whitaker."

March 15, 1991: "I went to see the sick and also the doctor." (This entry is a perfect example of personal sacrifices made by I.D. Back. Although he was ill enough to require a doctor visit himself, he was still trying to visit others who were sick and offer comfort to them.)

April 2, 1991: "I went to Neon for the funeral of A. Sue Fields. We went to the farm." ("The farm" is a reference to John Preece's Nicholasville farm.)

April 3, 1991: "On the farm. I went to see Brother Agnan and Sister M. Nichols."

April 4, 1991: "We come home today. I went to Everidge Funeral Home services for (?) Bowling." (The question mark indicates that the author could not decode this person's first name.)

April 22, 1991: " I was called at 3 o'clock this morning to come to Hazard Hospital to pray with M. Banks. Ina Rose and I went to get groceries and I mowed the lawn."

April 30, 1991: "I went to Arizona Holcomb's funeral and then to Hazard Hospital to see Brother Jack (Brown) and also to Elder J.W.'s church for visitation. And to see doctor. I went to Everidge Funeral Home service for Ada B."

May 2, 1991: "Tony and Jina gave us a precious little boy today. At 9:30 tonight. Thank God." (In this entry, I.D. is referring to the birth of his grandson, Anthony.)

May 20, 1991: "We kept Anthony for Jina today. I also went to see Brother Jack Brown. I went to Big Leatherwood Church for Essie Halcomb's funeral service."

June 30, 1991: "I went to our Association Building for services today. Also, I went to Little Carr Baptist Church to marry Joe Back and Lea. Also, went to Hazard Hospital to see Sister L. Smith. We have a grandbaby Anthony with us today. Our good friend M. Nichols died."

July 27, 1991: "I went to see Brother Jack Brown and also to our Association Building for our prayer of thanks to God for the ending of the war."

Aug. 22, 1991: "I went to the hospital, nursing home, and also to D. Pratt's funeral."

Sept. 8, 1991: "I went and introduced services at the association and went on to Hindman United Baptist Church for Mattie T.'s funeral."

Oct. 8, 1991: "I took Ina Rose to the doctor today. Also, I went to the hospital to see the sick and went to Letcher Funeral Home for visitation for Charles Whitaker."

Nov. 6, 1991: "I went to the hospital to see Aunt Critty and also to see Brother Jack Brown and went to help Tony to try to get a better job. 49 years ago today, Walton, Van, and me were sworn into the army at Fort Ben Harrison, Indiana."

Nov. 28, 1991: "Thanksgiving Day. We was all together.... Thank God. We ate at Sherry's. I went back to the hospital and nursing home. Also, to Letcher Funeral Home services for Allie (?) Tyree." (Question mark indicates that the author had difficulty decoding this person's first name and might have printed it incorrectly.)

Dec. 7, 1991: "50 years ago Japan bombed Pearl Harbor, started World War II. Sherry and Callie took Ina Rose shopping. I went to the hospital to see the sick. It was our church time. A good meeting."

Dec. 9, 1991: "I went and got car insurance. Also, to hospital and nursing home. Sister Nora Raleigh fell and broke her hip and arm. I had H. Cornett's funeral today."

Dec. 10, 1991: "I got sick and went to Dr. Artie Ann (Bates). She sent me on to the Hazard Hospital. I was put in intensive care."

Dec. 15, 1991: "I got out (of the hospital) today and come to Brother Jack Brown's funeral. Doc come after me." ("Doc" is a reference to I.D.'s son-in-law, Doc Fugate.)

Dec. 24, 1991: "It is Christmas Eve. Bro. Agnan and I went to Brashears' Funeral Home for the funeral of Kathleen Ison. We had all the family for Christmas Eve. Supper and exchange of gifts. We were so glad."

Near the end of the 1991 journal, there was a note citing various people's wedding anniversary dates. A few pages beyond that, there was a heading that read, "Baptizing 1991." Underneath that heading, the following names and dates were listed:
January 27- Randy Campbell
Feb. 3- Danny Campbell
Mar. 3 - B. Whitaker
Mar. 3 -Lane Campbell
Mar. 3- Willie Walters
Mar. 3- Jerrie Walters
Mar. 3- Bessie Smith

Mar. 17- Bill M.
Mar. 17- (unreadable first name) Crochton
Mar. 17- Linda Crochton
Apr. 21 - G. Combs
Apr. 21 - Genieva
Apr. 28 - Woodrow Whitaker
Apr. 28 - Q. Day
May 5- Beulah Back
May 12 - C. Jake Huff
June 9 - John L. Collins
July 21- Nancy C. Banks
July 21 - Dennis Ison
Aug. 11 - Renna Stidham
Sept. 15 - S. Slone
Sept. 22 - Hillard Caudill

A few pages later, there was another heading. This one read as follows: "1991 Funerals."
Under the heading is a list of names and dates. These are listed below.
Jan. 3 - Elsie Cornett Huff
Jan. 6- Flora Fields
Jan. 6 - Boyd Tolliver
Jan. 9 - Watson Caudill
Jan. 19 -Austin Miller
Jan. 22 - Homer Callahan
Jan. 26 - Lucian Cook
Jan. 30 - R. Cornett
Feb. 1 - Delmon Hayes
Feb. 2 - B. Gilley
Feb. 8 - W.B. Francis
Feb. 10 -Daniel Ritchie
Feb. 10 -Rena Faye P.
Mar. 1 - M.L. Caudill
Mar. 6 - William H. Richardson
Mar. 7 - W. Brashears
Mar. 8 - Dillard Pratt
Mar. 16- Glaydus Blair

Mar. 18 - Minerva Riddle
Mar. 24 - Thelma Cole
Mar. 26- Steve Adams
Mar. 28 - Michael S. Sparkman
Apr. 2 -O. Sue Fields
Apr. 7 - Jim S.
Apr. 30 - Ada Brown
May 4 - Betty Blair
May 10 -George Reynolds
May 12 - Mary E.
May 22 - Jean Stamper
May 23 - Luther M.
June 1 - Eddie T.
June 25 - Kermit Halcomb
July 7 - Jonah Caudill
July 18 - Rex Blair
July 28 - Earnest Sumpter
Aug. 5 - Millard Brown
Aug. 15 - Eugene Ison
Aug. 17 - Shirley Williams
Aug. 22 - Duke Pratt
Aug. 25 - John Whitaker
Sept. 1 - Laura Roark
Sept. 8 - Mattie Taylor
Sept. 9 - Effie Banks
Sept. 10 - Arlie Stamper
Sept. 18 - Mary Caudill
Sept. 29 - Elmon Potter
Sept. 29 - Myrtle Halcomb
Sept. 29 - M. Davidson
Oct. 9 - Charles Whitaker
Oct. 12 - Ival Ison
Oct. 13 - Dudley Whitaker
Oct. 27 - James Breeding
Nov. 3- Willie Blair
Nov. 12- Delma Cornett
Nov. 18 - Bob S.
Nov. 19 -Hoyt Cupps
Nov. 25 - Arlie Sexton

Nov. 28 - John Webb
Nov. 29 - Ollie Tyree
Dec. 4- Wanda K.
Dec. 9 - Howard Cornett
Dec. 24 - Kathleen Ison B.

Jan. 1, 1992: "Met at our church for our annual singing and was on our knees at 12 o'clock praying old year out and New Year in."

Jan. 24, 1992: "A snow storm this morning. I went to the doctor, and it seems I might have lung problems."

January 26, 1992: "I had a rough night. I was up different times and up at 5 to stay up. I went to Cedar Grove Church today."

(Entries recorded throughout much of Feb. 1992 address the fact that I.D. is still very ill. Still, he often manages to insert comments about the well-being of his family members, as well as comments about whether or not he was able to attend church services on a given day.)

Feb. 26, 1992: "My son Tony called me this morning. It was so good to hear him. I went to my dr. today at Hazard. Ina Rose and I ate out. I went to Letcher Funeral Home for Jim Back's funeral."

Feb. 27, 1992: "I went to Bro. Jim Back's funeral and went got a haircut, and went to get Sherry and bring her home. I got to see Anthony."

[The two entries above attest to the fact that, as soon as I.D. had recuperated (or recuperated in part, at least), he would immediately return to his routine of caring for his family and doing the work of God.]

March 14, 1992: "I went to Little Dove Church this morning. Also went to Mayking Church for Noble

Bates' funeral. Also, at the First Baptist Church, I married Greg and Maxine C., and come home to our church - funeral for D.W."

March 22, 1992: "We had the funeral of Sister Vina Pratt Fields. Also, my heart took a spell of beating too fast."

March 26, 1992: "I went to Pic Pac for Tony and Jina. I went to see the baby, and also went to the hospital and nursing home to see the sick."

April 18, 1992: "I went to see Steve W., and Amos Collins this morning, and I went this evening to Hazard Hospital to see a good friend E. Adams. Also to Blair Branch Church."

April 29, 1992: "I went to see Lucky Banks today. I went to Letcher Funeral Home service for Carlos Bates."

Sept. 1, 1992: "I went to Letcher Funeral Home for the funeral of Beulah Hampton. Ina Rose and I, Sherry and Doc, Callie, Tony, and Jina all went to funeral home visitation for Lester Lusk."

Sept. 2, 1992: "I went to Lester Lusk's funeral. Also went to help clean our Association Building. Got Anthony a stroller."

Sept. 21, 1992: "I got a new car today. Also had the funeral for Hanna B."

Oct. 4, 1992: "It was our church time. I went over and then I went to Letcher Funeral Home for Bro. Marion Day's funeral and also to Bro. Agnan's 79th birthday and also to Sister Oma B. L.'s for prayer for her. She has cancer."

Nov. 1, 1992: "I went to our Association building for church today. Come back to Blair Branch for the baptizing Sister Jo Ann Walters and ate with them. I went on to the hospital to see Katie Griffin...and others. Ina Rose has been sick today."

Nov. 10, 1992: "I stayed around home most of the day. I have felt bad. I went to see S. Watts and Vina Pratt and Arnold Blair who are sick."

Nov. 26, 1992: "Thanksgiving - I went to see Stevie Watts and Amos Collins. We ate at Sherry and Doc's. Ina Rose helped cook. We are very thankful. God is good."

Dec. 7, 1992: "Would have been Walton's birthday. Also, 51 years ago, Pearl Harbor was bombed. I went to Letcher Funeral Home. Funeral for D. Ison. Also went to John B.'s, and he joined the church, and then I went to Hazard Hospital to see Brother Herman Adams."

Dec. 16, 1992: "I left the Hurricane Forest and the Battle of the Bulge 45 years ago today. I went to see the sick and shop. I also went to the dr., and I am sick." (Upon reading over a draft form of this manuscript, Ronnie had written a correction that needed to be made in regard to this entry. His comment read, "Hurtgen Forest. Pap could never get that right." The author thought that both I.D.'s mistake, and the comment that Ronnie had written about correcting it, were endearing.)

Jan. 1, 1993: "It was a great time at our church. Prayer at midnight and great meeting. We went to Whitesburg. Ina Rose and myself ate out. I went to see Bro. Agnan, Sister V. Adams. Also went to see Bro. Elmer and Ruby at Irishman Creek. We went to see Tony, Jina, and boys."

Feb. 10, 1993: "I went to Hindman Funeral Home today for OB Sorrell's funeral. I went on to Hazard to the hospital to see Mason Caudill, V. Adams, Stevie Watts, Bro. Jim Pratt. Also today Bro. Monroe Caudill died. Darlene Watts called and said God had saved her soul and wanted to join the church. Brother Danny Dixon, Brother Don Halcomb, Brother Elwood Cornett, Brother Jim Fields was there. We took her into the church...."

March 6, 1993: "I went to Everidge Funeral Home for the funeral of John T. I took Ina Rose to Hazard and went to see Bro. Coy Fields, Bill, and Brother Kirby Jent. We ate out. It was our church time. Brother James Caudill and Nina his wife came into our church. A great meeting."

March 20, 1993: "I went to see Bro. Agnan at the hospital. He is real low. Also went to Aunt L. Smith's 100th birthday. A real sad time. While at Blair Branch Church, the news came that Bro. Agnan had died. A great soldier of the Cross." (Author's note: Agnan "Ag" Back was an Old Regular Baptist minister, who had preached alongside I.D. for many years. Mention was made of him in an earlier chapter of this book, as he had also served as the clerk at Mt. Olivet Old Regular Baptist Church for several years. He was a very humble man, who was small in stature, had snow-white hair, and often wore a fedora into the church house. Sometimes, in his preaching, he would become so overtaken by the good feeling of God's Spirit that he would run, skip, or jump on the stand, despite the fact that he was far from being a young man. He was a jewel of a human being, and, over the years, he and I.D. had become very close friends.)

March 23, 1993: "We had Bro. Agnan Back's funeral today. He had many, many friends. After the funeral, Ina Rose and I went to the farm."

March 24, 1993: "On the farm and Annabelle Wright called me that her mother had died."

March 26, 1993: "We come home today and we had J. Wright's funeral today. I don't feel just right somehow."

April 12, 1993: "We went to Whitesburg - shopped and ate out. Went to see Verna. She is so lonesome.... Sherry and Doc took Callie to get her award for drawing. I am so proud of her. Also, Ronnie made (a) on his ... test. I am proud of him. He and Hester left for Lexington for her test. I pray all will be well." (In referring to "Verna," I.D. is making reference to Agnan Back's widow.)

April 13, 1993: "I went to my dr. - got a good report. I went to see Bro. Carson Cornett, L.C., also Stevie Watts, who told me it was well with his soul."

May 24, 1993: "I went to Cedar Grove Church for Sarah Ison funeral. Also back to Cedar Grove services for Laura Roark. Worked hard around home."

May 25, 1993: "I went and voted. Took Callie to Whitesburg with me. Went to Cedar Grove Church for L. Roark's funeral."

June 12, 1993: "I went to Rudell Blair's home and married Bro. Lowell Caudill's daughter to Greg Sturgill. Also, on to Doty and married Chris Ison and Marie Parks. Also to graveside service for B.C. Stop to visit Dr. Adams."

July 4, 1993: "I was 68-years-old today. It was church time and memorial meeting. Brother Glenn gave me dinner money, and I took Ina Rose to Hazard to eat. Also, I went to the Letcher Funeral Home for Betty Jo P.'s funeral. Sherry had cake and ice cream for me."

Aug. 5, 1993: "I went to my Dr., today, and had blood work done. I went to see Brother Jim Pratt."

Aug. 6, 1993: "I went to the hospital to see V., and also the nursing home to see Hester and L. Branson, and it was time for the bread baking for our church for Sacrament."

Aug. 10, 1993: "I went to Morgan County to see Brother Wardie Craft and had a great day. He is very sick. A great man. Has preached for 65 years."

Aug. 15, 1993: "I went out on the mountain where Bro. Agnan was buried for church and also went to Defeated Creek for Communion. And also to Letcher Funeral Home for E. Breeding funeral." (When I.D. refers in this entry to going "out on the mountain," he is making reference to the location of a cemetery on Elk Creek Mountain. That is, indeed, where Agnan Back is buried, and I.D. was going there in order to attend an annual memorial service.)

Sept. 3, 1993: "I went to our Association today. Good preachin'. I went to see Watson Combs in trouble over his sins."

Sept. 4, 1993: "I went to the Association this morning and went on to Clyde Creech funeral at Manchester and went on to London to see Ruth. Came home to our home church." ("Ruth" was I.D.'s sister.)

Oct. 2, 1993: "I went to Dixon Memorial funeral for George Bryant. I also came to our church for Winford Watts's funeral."

Nov. 24, 1993: "I took Callie to school this morning. I worked on the hedges, and I went to see Sister Nora Raleigh, and also to the hospital and the nursing home and see Bro. John Brown. And also went to Kingdom Come Church funeral service for Brother Jack Back."

Nov. 25, 1993: "This is Thanksgiving, and we ate at Sherry and Doc's. Mae ate with us. We went to Hazard. I went to see R. Combs. Tony come over and Byron come in from Indiana." (The mention of "Mae" is made in reference to Sherry's mother-in-law, Mae Fugate.)

Nov. 29, 1993: "I went to Whitesburg to get Ina Rose medicine. I also went to Vicco Baptist Church for Mack B.'s funeral. I went to Corbett Brashear's funeral service at his church. A great host of people paid respects to a good man."

Dec. 3, 1993: "I went to Leatherwood Clinic to get Ina Rose medicine. Then, I went to Cedar Grove Church for Bessie Carter's funeral and also went to Letcher Funeral Home for Ruby Combs's funeral service. I went with Brother Jr. Lusk and Mildred." (Jr. and Mildred Lusk were both members of the Mt. Olivet Old Regular Baptist Church, and they had a close relationship with I.D. and Ina Rose. Many people refer to Jr., who is still living today, as "Poppy." I can remember hearing I.D. refer to him as "Poppy Doo!" At other times, he referred to June and Mildred as "Poppy Doll" and "Mommy Doll.")

Jan. 1, 1994: "I went to Cedar Grove Church for the funeral of Sister E. Griffie. Also went to her burying. I took Ina Rose out for supper on New Year's Day. It was our church time, and a good one it was."

Jan. 4, 1994: "There is another snow storm this morning. We had Sister (Hester) Back's funeral today at our church. I went to the grave. It was a beautiful time with the white snow."

Feb. 23, 1994: "We went to Cincinnati for the funeral of Little Amber. It sure was sad. We come to Nicholasville and spent the night."

Feb. 28, 1994: "Tony come home today. I went to see Brother Wayne Cole in the hospital. Also went to get Ina Rose's medicine and had my tooth filled. I went to B. Blair's home for services for his wife who had joined the church."

March 4, 1994: "I went to Watson Adams's funeral at Isom. Also, I went to take part in George Smith's funeral. Also, I visited Troy Back and his wife. I went to Letcher Funeral Home services for Brother Junior Lusk's aunt, Susannah Banks."

April 30, 1994: "I went to Mason's Creek to marry Rick Adams's sister and also to Hurricane Gap Church."

May 7, 1994: "I had the funeral of Susan C. - also of G. Ritchie. Also, I married Dorse Fields's son to Frank Fouts's daughter and went to my church. Also went to visit the hospital - my sick friends."

June 2, 1994: "I took Tony to work and went to the hospital to see the sick. Also, went back to Whitesburg for services for M. Whitaker and went back to the hospital, and rehearsed a wedding."

July 4, 1994: "I was 69-years-old today. Ina Rose and I went to Buckhorn State Resort Park and ate. All my children wished me a happy birthday. I went to Engle Funeral Home for J.K.'s funeral service."

(Much of August 1994's entries focused upon Ina Rose being in ICU and having heart surgery.)

Sept. 14, 1994: "I stayed with Ina Rose until Callie came home and then I go to Jina in the hospital. Also, I saw Thelma C., and John Watts and others."

Sept. 19, 1994: "I went to Brother John Brown's wife - lost his son in a tractor wreck. Brother Roy Miller and his good wife come to see Ina Rose - brought a beautiful bird feeder. Tony came over. Ray Back called, and Loni Campbell was operated on."

Oct. 25, 1994: "I went to Leatherwood Clinic for medicine. Also went to see Brother Holbert Collins and on to a dr. appointment. I found out I have black lung. I also went to see my friend Amos Collins."

Nov. 1, 1994: "I took Ina Rose to her doctor. I also went to see Dr. Adams, a friend who is not well."

Dec. 24, 1994: "I went to Jeff for graveside service for Herman C."

Dec. 25, 1994: "I went to Cedar Grove Church Service. Brother Danny Dixon preached a great sermon."

Jan. 1, 1995: "We were on our knees at our church at midnight from (19) 94 to (19) 95."

Jan. 2, 1995: "I have been sick and missed church. I hope to do better."

Feb. 13, 1995: "Sherry took Tony to work, and I took Callie to school, and also went to Blair Branch Church for Laura Caudill's funeral. I went and got Tony from work and he ate with us. Brother Virgil Combs and I went to Little Cowan Church for Dixon Fields's funeral."

March 5, 1995: "We got to keep Anthony again last night. It was church time. We had a joiner. A great meeting. I went to see Brother Bill W. and wife."

April 9, 1995: "I went to Defeated Creek Church today. A great time. Glenna Caudill joined the church. I also went to Big Cowan and also to see Dr. Lundy Adams. Sung him 3 songs."

May 24, 1995: "I took Tony to work. I went to Cedar Grove Church for Sister George Anne Watts's funeral, and also went to Letcher Funeral Home services for B. Whitaker."

June 4, 1995: "I went to our church. A good meeting. Sister Martha Caudill died today. I went over to be with the family. We have our baby Anthony."

July 16, 1995: "It was Blair Branch Church time and Communion. Many...joined the church. A great day. I went to the hospital to see Brother Critty and others. Also to the funeral home service for Bill Gibson's sister."

Aug. 4, 1995: "We had our boy Anthony and his dad messed up again. We had our baking of bread at the church for our Communion."

Sept. 13, 1995: "I took Ina Rose to Hazard. We got Anthony's pictures and went to Lexington to the hospital - Central Baptist - to see Brother Merle Smith."

Oct. 2, 1995: "I went to see F. Couch. Also to Little Dove for Brother Merle Smith's funeral. Came home and got Ina Rose and took her to her doctor. A good night. We ate out."

Nov. 6, 1995: "53 years ago I joined the army. I went to Hazard Hospital to see V. Cornett."

Nov. 12, 1995: "I went to the hospital to see Lester Gibson and also the nursing home and on to Cedar Grove service for "Bucket" Griffie. Took Brother Boyd Caudill with me."

Dec. 16, 1995: "Tony and I took Anthony to Wal-Mart. Ate out. I went to Letcher Funeral Home service for D. Collins. Stopped at Blair Branch Church. I got news that I had a slipped disc and a pinched nerve in my neck."

Dec. 24, 1995: "I went to Tolson Church. A great service. We went to Ronnie and Hester's for our Christmas supper."

Dec. 31, 1995: "I stayed home and could not go to church and...Wright funeral."

Jan. 1, 1996: "Ina Rose and myself got on our knees and prayed. I also had to go to Dr. Caudill today. Ronnie took me."

[There were no entries recorded between January 5 and January 21, 1996. On the 21st of January, I.D. had written, "I have been sick in the hospital 18 days. I am home now still in bad shape with my hip. Come home the 21st." Throughout the remainder of Jan. 1996, the journal entries focus mostly upon the fact that I.D. is still sick and "shut in." Still, he managed to note the days on which several special friends (Critty Stewart, Junior Yonts, John Halcomb) died.]

Feb. 6, 1996: "I am still housed in. I feel stronger each day. Thank God. Well, they buried Bonnie Duke today. Another dear friend."

March 2, 1996: "I went to Rodney Ison's. Serviced our car. I got to go to my church tonight. The first time in 2 months. I thank God for helping me. I got to go to church last night. A good one...."

April 1, 1996: "Tony and I took Anthony to school and went on to Prestonsburg. We have had snow today. KY won the NCAA tour."

April 6, 1996: "Callie is 13-years-old today. I went to Victor 'Big' Campbell's. Hope had surgery on gallstones. S. Wright's wife died last night - the mother of our circuit judge Sam Wright. Callie is having a great party with her friends. Sherry brought Sydney by. She is so pretty. I went to our church, and it was a good one." (In mentioning "Hope," I.D. was referring to Victor Campbell's wife. Mention of "Sydney" was made in reference to I.D.'s great-granddaughter, Sydney Back, who would have been less than one-year-old at the time that this journal entry was written.)

April 11, 1996: "I had a bad morning. Got some better and went to Tri-City Funeral Home for Bill W.'s funeral. Came home and Tony called and G. Wright died, from being run over by a tractor and trailor. I also went to Mitchell's tonight."

May 3, 1996: "I had the fast heart beat last night. I went to Letcher Funeral Home visitation for Sister Essie Caudill."

May 4, 1996: "I went to Letcher Funeral Home for the funeral of Sister Essie Caudill. My back still hurts. It is church time at home. A good service. Tony called us today. It was good to hear his voice."

May 24, 1996: "I took Ina Rose to her doctor. I went back to Wh., to go to the funeral home, but felt I better come home. Ronnie has mowed both graveyards. My friend George Watts died. I had to go in the hospital."

May 25 and 26, 1996 entries read as follows: "In the hospital."

July 20, 1996: "I have had a fair day. Ina Rose feels real bad. Brother Rodney come and got me and took me to Blair Branch Church. The church presented me with a plaque for serving the church as moderator for 20 years. I was glad and thankful."

Aug. 4, 1996: "I had a bad ½ day. First half was bad, but Sherry took me and her mother to our church for Communion, and it was great. Shirley and Ron brought Sydney up."

Sept. 5, 1996: "I have had another bad day. Brother 'Big' Campbell called me. I was glad. Also, Sister Bessie A died. A great member of our Little Dove Church."

Sept. 11, 1996: "It has been a fair day. Ronnie took me to Alma Fields's house. It was hard and sad. She is so hurt over the death of Donnie. Troy Jent called."
(Author's note: Donnie Fields, my mother's brother, was killed in a car accident on the evening of September 10, 1996. Alma Fields is my maternal grandmother. This entry refers to one of the many times that I.D. helped our family through a sorrowful situation.)

Sept. 12, 1996: "Ronnie, Hester, Sherry, and myself went to the funeral home to pay respects to Donnie Fields's family."

Sept. 17-Sept. 29, 1996: "Hazard Hospital"

Nov. 3, 1996: "It was church time, and at home. I got to go. We had a joiner. Brother Adams. A great service. Ronnie went to church."

Jan. 1, 1999: "We met at our church time and sang and prayed until midnight. We had a good time in the Lord. Today, Hester is down with her back. Tony called today."

Jan. 2, 1999: "I have a problem this morning of bleeding. Ronnie went and got our mail. Brother Paul Sparkman and Benton Campbell brought me a big fresh shoulder sliced. It was church time at home and a great meeting. Brother Bill Halcomb was with us."

Jan. 3, 1999: I was bleeding this morning and was afraid to go to church."

Jan. 5, 1999: "A real cold night. Ronnie came and got our mail for us. I went to Letcher Funeral Home services for Shelby Jean Adams. Sherry stayed with her mother for me."

Jan. 7, 1999: "It's been a fair day, a little warmer. I went to the Letcher Funeral Home. Visitation Edna Back. Ronnie stayed with his mother for me. Doc drove me home."

Jan. 10, 1999: "went to Little Dove Church, a great service. Ivan and Freddie done real well. Sherry stayed with her mother for me. Nancy sent us some good soup. Sister Mildred Tiller brought cake, ...fish, and deer meat." (The name "Nancy" likely refers to Nancy Oaks, Ina Rose's niece. The names "Ivan" and "Freddie" likely refer to Elder Ivan Amburgey and Elder Fred Frazier. Mildred Tiller is the daughter of I.D.'s longtime friend, John Preece.)

Jan. 20, 1999: "Tony called this morning. Ronnie has to stay another day and night in the hospital. I went to Little Dove for the funeral of Brother Roy Miller. Brother John come and preached."

Feb. 23, 1999: "A bad day for me and Ina Rose. Brother Chester Brown had heart surgery today. I called about Brother John at the farm."

Feb. 25, 1999: "I went to the grocery and also to the bank. Ina Rose was not able to go to the doctor today.... Just got word that Brother John's cancer is in remission. Thank God. Sad news - Sister Linda Watts having brain surgery now. God help her."

(Author's note: God did help Linda Watts, wife of Freddie Lane "Soup Bean" Watts. She had an aneurism in her brain, and the doctors gave her a very slim chance of survival. Even if she did survive, the doctors had warned Freddie that she would never be the same. A lot of prayers went up for her, however. Today, she walks and talks and functions pretty much the same way that she did before the surgery. She's a walking miracle, and, undoubtedly, I.D.'s prayers were helpful in making that outcome happen.)

Feb. 27, 1999: "Doc and Sherry went to Smoky Mt., on their anniversary. I called the Baptist hospital and talked to Brother Chester Brown."

Feb. 28, 1999: "I did not get to go to church Sunday. I called Brother Glenn and Brother John. Heard from Brother Chester Brown and Linda Watts. Tony called."

April 9, 1999: "I went to the doctor today. I had lost 10 pounds. Also got a brace. Dr. Breeding told me Brother Glenn has a very short time. Tony called his mother. Ronnie and Hester go on their vacation tomorrow. I am glad for them." ("Glenn" is in reference to I.D.'s good friend, Glenn Hampton.)

April 16, 1999: "One of our best friends Brother Glenn died around 3 o'clock. I went to Letcher Funeral Home service for Burley Back."

April 19, 1999: "Tony called us today. We were so glad. I went to the grocery and stopped at Brother Glenn's house to see his family."

April 20, 1999: "Another school shooting in Colorado. They say 25 has been killed. It's a sad time."

April 23, 1999: "I took Ina Rose to her doctor, and she was put in the hospital to take blood...."

April 24, 1999: "I went to see Ina Rose today. She is not doing any good. Ronnie and Sherry was there. Also, I picked up our T.V. I went to Letcher Funeral Home service for Sister V. Sumpter. Also, back to see Ina Rose."

May 8, 1999: "It was church time at Little Dove. I did not get to go. No one to stay with Ina Rose."

May 24, 1999: "A real treat this morning. A young buck deer come in our yard. It was beautiful."

May 25, 1999: "I went and got a hair cut and went and got my iron shot. Sister Mary Adams died today. I went to see Joe Begley, a very sick man."

May 27, 1999: "I went to Everidge Funeral Home service for Sister M. Adams. 100-years-old. Got sick....and got bad off. The children helped me."

May 28, 1999: "I went to the doctor, and he put me in the hospital. Sherry come to me."

July 4, 1999: "I am 74-years-old today. I am by the Grace and mercy of God. Doc and Sherry brought us a good dinner. Byron called from Indiana and sang to me. Ike and Ronnie was here. Tony called last night. Kell called this morning. I have had a great day. I thank God for it."

Aug. 30, 1999: "Avis Stewart (Tab) died this morning. A neighbor and friend. I also went to get our medicine and groceries. I called about Brother John. It was not too good."

Sept. 5, 1999: "I went to Letcher Funeral Home for the funeral of Edd R. Also, Sister Madge Brown was baptized today. Ina Rose doing very well. Our little friend Paul Reed died."

Sept. 12, 1999: "I went to Little Dove and had a great meeting. Laid hands on Brother Green Watts's daughter. Tootsie and Willie went home today. I got another fast heart beat."

Sept. 16, 1999: "We took Ina Rose to see her doctor. Also ate out. A good and pretty day. I went to Anthony at school. Had lunch with him. It was Grandparents' Day. I went to Letcher Funeral Home service for Elbert Lee Caudill. Sherry stayed with her mother."

Sept. 25, 1999: "Byron, his wife, and Morgan came in from Indiana. I went to the Letcher Funeral Home service for Brother John P. Eldridge." (Byron is Ronnie Back's older son. His wife's name is Kristi. Morgan is their daughter, which would make her the great-granddaughter of I.D. and Ina Rose.)

Sept. 28, 1999: "One of our good members of Blair Branch Church died....We got some rain this morning. Joyce just called and told me that Brother John's time is short." ("Joyce" is Joyce Kitchen, one of John Preece's daughters.)

Oct. 7, 1999: "Today is Ronnie's birthday. 51-years-old. A special son. We had the funeral of Ben Caudill today. Burying him behind our house."

Oct. 8, 1999: "I went to see Brother John. He is so low - never did move or know me. Tony called his mother this morning. Brother John died at 10:15."

Oct. 10, 1999: "We had the funeral of Tessie Caudill today. A good crowd."

Oct. 12, 1999: "It was the funeral of my friend and brother John Preece. There was another huge crowd."

Oct. 13, 1999: "I went to Everidge Funeral Home for the funeral of Clyde Polly. Also, a nurse came by to see Ina Rose. A nice day. Tony sent money and said to tell Anthony he loves him a lot."

Nov. 19, 1999: "The Hospice people came by today, and Ina Rose was signed up on it."

Nov. 21, 1999: "I went to the Blair Branch Church and also to Little Dove for the funeral of Sister Norma A. Ronnie stayed with Ina Rose."

Nov. 27, 1999: "The nurse came to see Ina Rose. I cooked and fried my first rabbit today. I went to Tolson Church for the ordaining of Brother Virgil Caudill."

Nov. 29, 1999: "I went to the doctor and had two shots in the hip. Ina Rose seems some better. Bob Blair is very sick. Bill Adams some better."

Dec. 4, 1999: "I went to Little Dove and married David and Lisa Maggard. Also - our bake sale at church (had) a good turn-out. They sent Ina Rose a good dinner. It was church time at home. A good service. Ronnie stayed with his mother."

Dec. 5, 1999: "I went to our church. A good service. Shirley and Sidney and Andrew (and) Sherry and Doc come to church. Ronnie stayed with his mother." (Andrew is the son of Ikey and Shirley Back.)

Dec. 7, 1999: "I went to the post office and grocery and bank today. The nurses come by to see Ina Rose. I went to Isom Presbyterian Church service for Sister Allie Breeding."

Dec. 10 and 11, 1999: "Stayed home with Ina Rose."

Dec. 12, 1999: "I went to Little Dove and Brother H. Hall brought our dinner. Sherry stayed with her mother."

Dec. 13, 1999: "Ina Rose's nurse come to see her today. I took our car and had it fixed at Rodney's. I went to Letcher Funeral Home service for Brother R. Fields."

Dec. 18, 1999: "I stayed with Ina Rose, and I went to Blackey for a program for our children and had prayer with them."

Dec. 24, 1999: "We having a big snow. I called Kell and Elbert Hampton and Sister D. Whitaker. They lost their son Terry."

Dec. 25, 1999: "We have a nice snow on the ground. I fixed Ina Rose's Christmas for her, and, then, I went to Letcher Funeral Home service for Terry Whitaker."

"The last day of 1999: We had our singing at our church. I come home to be with Ina Rose. We thank God for it all."

"January 1 (the first day of 2000): I went to Danny Shepherd's and married his son Shan. Callie drove me there and back."

Jan. 2, 2000: "I went to our church, and it was great preaching and a huge congregation. Peanut and his wife joined Bruce Gilley's church today. I also went to Bull Creek Church."

Jan. 3, 2000: "I went to the bank. I also paid our bills. The nurse is come to Ina Rose."

Jan. 5, 2000: "Paul brought Ina Rose some pork chops. Phyllis and I cleaned on the house. Ina Rose about the same." ("Paul" is Paul Sparkman. "Phyllis" is family friend, Phyllis Asher.)

Jan. 9, 2000: "Ina Rose had chest pain, and I stayed home with her. Ronnie, Sherry, Doc, and Callie all was with her. I went to Rock Fork Church."

Jan. 10, 2000: "I went to Letcher Funeral Home for the funeral of Sister Pauline Shepherd. The nurse come to Ina Rose."

Jan. 13, 2000: "I have had a headache most of the day. Ina Rose not too good. I went to Everidge Funeral Home services for Brother George S."

Jan. 15, 2000: "I went to the Letcher Funeral Home. Funeral for Clyde Gilley. I been around the rest of the day. Ina Rose is better today."

Jan. 19, 2000: "Ina Rose fell in the floor. Doc had to come and get her up. She was not hurt. Thank God. The nurse has come to bathe her."

Jan. 21, 2000: "The Hospice chaplain come by and had prayer for Ina Rose. The nurse came and bathed Ina

Rose. Rodney Ison came and took me to Dixon Memorial Church for Sister Lucy's (Lucy Back) service."

Jan. 22, 2000: "I went to Dixon Memorial Church for the funeral of Sister Lucy Back. We had another snow. Brother Elwood and Sister Kathy brought us a ham and other goodies."

Jan. 23, 2000: "It's a nice snow on the ground. I called Brother Paul Sparkman at the hospital this morning. Sherry fixed a big dinner for us all. Ina Rose not too well tonight."

Feb. 1, 2000: "I went to Letcher Funeral Home for the service for John Banks. Also, the nurse came to see Ina Rose."

Feb. 2, 2000: "The groundhog saw his shadow. A neighbor got killed in Lexington this morning. Sister Sarah Watts's grandson. The nurse came to see Ina Rose."

Feb. 8, 2000: "The nurses came to see Ina Rose today. I went to Everidge Funeral Home service for Sister Bonnie Pratt. Ronnie stayed with his mother."

Feb. 10, 2000: "I went to Bull Creek Church for the funeral of Sister Dessie Combs. Ronnie stayed with his mother."

Feb. 13, 2000: "I went to Little Dove Church. We had great preaching. Ronnie stayed with his mother. I got Ina Rose a good dinner. She has felt better today. Thank God. Sister Mary Lou Blair, Brother Manis and Sister Mary Ison's daughter, died. A great loss."

Feb. 14, 2000: "It's a sad day for us all. The loss of Mary Lou. Ina Rose's nurse came to see her today."

Feb. 15, 2000: "I went to Letcher School to see, and be with, Anthony. I saw and went to his class. I was proud of him. The nurse come to see Ina Rose today. I went to Letcher Funeral Home for service for Sister Mary Lou Blair."

Feb. 18, 2000: "We had to get an ambulance to take Ina Rose to the clinic and back. The nurse is with her now."

Feb. 19, 2000: "Brother Fred Adams died today. Sister Oma Lewis is real sick. I went to Blair Branch Church and had a wonderful time in the Lord. Brother Frank Newsome was there."

Feb. 22, 2000: "The nurse and preacher both were here today to see Ina Rose. I went to the funeral home service for Sister Oma Bates Lewis."

March 1, 2000: "The nurse come to see Ina Rose today. I went to get the mail. It's a windy March day, but nice. Brother Charles Amburgey died last night. Rosco P. Smith died today. Ina Rose not doing too good."

March 3, 2000: "I went to Letcher Funeral Home for the funeral of Rosco Smith and also to Blair Branch Church for the funeral of Brother Charles Amburgey."

March 4, 2000: "I am up at 4 o'clock this morning. I went to the bank this morning. Ronnie stayed with Ina Rose. The Miller girls (Pee Wee and Renee) come to see us and brought us a lot of good food. Elbert Hampton and Edgar Whitaker came to see us. It was our church time tonight. James Caudill brought us a lot of good food. God bless them all."

March 8-12, 2000: "in the hospital"

March 13, 2000: "I got home today from the hospital."

March 15, 2000: "I am having a bad day. So is Ina Rose. It's so beautiful outside. The nurse came to bathe Ina Rose. Ronnie had to take me to the doctor."

March 16, 2000: "I am better today. Not too strong. Ina Rose not too well."

March 26, 2000: "I stayed home with Ina Rose. We had a pretty fair day. Sherry checks on us. It was a beautiful day. The Lord's Day."

March 27, 2000: "I went to my doctor today. My friend Joe Begley died today. Ina Rose not too well. Paul Sparkman took me to the doctor."

March 28, 2000: "...I went to the funeral home service for Joe Begley."

March 29, 2000: "I went to the graveyard for graveside services for Joe Begley. Jina and Doc came to see Ina Rose."

April 1, 2000: "I stayed with Ina Rose all day and went to our church. A good meeting. Brother Jim Fields preached real good. Ronnie stayed with his mother."

April 2, 2000: "I went to our church. A great service. Brother Danny done so good. She had company. Cleo and J." ("She" is in reference to Ina Rose.)

April 19, 2000: "Ronnie stayed with me and his mother last night. I tried to get Ina Rose up, and I hurt my back. Ina Rose not too well."

April 24, 2000: "I went to the doctor and got 2 shots for my back. Ina Rose got real low today. Sherry, Doc, and Callie are with us. Tony called and he made it back."

April 25, 2000: "Ina Rose is very ill today. I was told the time is short. Brother James Caudill, Brother Elwood and Cathy, Ray and Beulah all came to see her. Sherry, Paul's daughter, has helped us today." (In this case, "Sherry" is in reference to one of the Hospice workers, who is also the daughter or Paul and Dee Wee Sparkman.)

April 26, 2000: "A bad night for Ina Rose. Ronnie and Hester got here at 6 o'clock. Ina Rose went home to Heaven about 8:30. She went to sleep in the arms of Jesus."

April 27, 2000: "We all went to the funeral home for the service for her. It was so good."

April 28, 2000: "Today was the funeral for Ina Rose. It was special. Danny and Elwood was blessed so wonderfully. We went to the grave with her. We left her there and angels to watch over her. Now I sit here all alone. Lonesome and sad. She has gone to be with Jesus."

April 29, 2000: "Another lonely day. The children has come to be with me. Ronnie took me to the grave. It was so pretty up there. Doc and Sherry just left to their house."

April 30, 2000: "I went to church today. A good meeting. Came to a lonely house and my friend Brad Bentley come to see me with a great gift."

May 2, 2000: "I went to the grave of Ina Rose. Ronnie took me. It's hard."

May 3, 2000: "I went to the post office. Also to the bank and drug store. I miss her very much."

May 4, 2000: "I went to town. Also to visit P. Cornett. Sherry came and brought my supper. I miss her so much."

May 5, 2000: "I went to the funeral of sister Elizabeth M. Today. I went to Letcher Funeral Home visitation for V. Smith."

May 6, 2000: "I went to Letcher Funeral Home for the funeral of Vernon Smith. Also, Sherry and I went to Ina Rose's grave."

May 7, 2000: "I went to our church. A good meeting. Sherry and Doc come up a while tonight. I went to Ina Rose's grave. Took some snowballs to the grave."

May 8, 2000: "I went to the doctor. Also to the bank. Brother Danny Terry come over and went to the grave with me. See where to set the stones. Big Keith Mullins brought me fish, hush puppies, and strawberry cake."

May 9, 2000: "I was so sad this morning. I could hardly make it, and all the sudden Tony come around the house. It's so good to see him. I went to Isom to eat. Phyllis and her friend come to see us. Also Jim Keller. He goes tomorrow on a big trip. My good friend Bill Ison died today."

May 13, 2000: "I went to Little Dove Church. A good service. My back is in bad shape. Sherry come up and stayed with me late last night."

May 14, 2000: "I went back to Little Dove for Sunday meeting. It was union meeting. A good day. Sherry and Ronnie came by. It was Mother's Day. They were so hurt."

May 15, 2000: "I stayed around home all day. Tony came by. Also Ronnie and Sherry. I have had a better day, but is not the same anymore."

May 16, 2000: "I went to the grave this morning. I also went to Wal-Mart and the drug store. Sue had her baby today. We are all so happy." ("Sue" refers to Sue Fugate, wife of Doc's son, Allen. The baby referred to was named "Ashton.")

May 18, 2000: "We all went to see our new baby. Allen and Sue has a beautiful baby boy. (I miss her bad.)"

May 19, 2000: "They put up our tombstone today. It is so beautiful. Ellis Cornett went on the hill with me. I am having a bad time with my back."

May 20, 2000: "I am down with my back. Also am spitting up blood. Brother Jamie L. (?), and his wife, come to see me. Sherry has been up ½ day." (Question mark indicates that the author was unsure as to whether or not I.D. meant for this to be the letter "L".)

May 21, 2000: "I went to Blair Branch Church today. Had a good meeting. I have felt some better."

May 23, 2000: "Tony took me to vote. I went to Whitesburg for a Catscan. Got a little dizzy at Pic-Pac. Callie took care of me. We ate out. Our man Mike Caudill won his race."

May 28, 2000: "I went to Cedar Grove for Memorial Meeting. A great service. Also a good dinner. Brother Eddie Howard died today. He fell over his mother's grave."

May 29, 2000: I went to Mayking Church for a funeral...Ate at Lee's Restaurant. Come and went on the hill to Ina Rose's grave."

May 30, 2000: "I put out a washing and ironing and trimmed the hedges. Hester brought my meal to me. I went to the First Baptist Church for service for Brother Eddie Howard. A great man."

May 31, 2000: "I went to the doctor today. Come home for the rest of the day. I sure did miss Ina Rose today."

June 1, 2000: "I went to Hindman today to the office.... A good visit. I ate a dessert at the restaurant. (I miss her.)" ("The restaurant" likely refers to the dining place inside the Holly Hills Shopping Center. This shopping center is named in honor of John Preece's daughter, Holly.)

June 3, 2000: "Ronnie and I went to the grave. There was two deer in the grave yard. It was our churchtime. A good service. I miss her bad."

June 12, 2000: "I went into the hospital today."

June 27, 2000: "I finally got home today, but had to turn around and go back when I fell. I am home at last. Thank God."

CHAPTER 30
Home At Last

When reading the journal entries recorded in the previous chapter, the reader will note that, especially in latter entries, it is evident that, other than God, Jesus, and the Holy Ghost, Ina Rose Back was the most important being in I.D. Back's life. No matter what he had done on a given day or how he himself felt physically, he rarely failed to write some comment regarding Ina Rose's physical condition. After her death, he often wrote of the fact that he missed her. He might, for example, have written something as simple as, "I miss her bad." The word "her" generally needed no further explanation, because the "her" to which he was referring was the one great love of his life.

Yet, for all the love that I.D. felt for Ina Rose, he felt an even greater love for, and a stronger devotion to, God. In reading through his journals, I was amazed by the number of entries in which he would refer to illness afflicting himself and/or his family members, and then, in that same entry (or soon thereafter), make mention of being at a funeral or a church service or somewhere else (e.g., visiting the sick) where he could be doing the Lord's work. Even on holidays and birthdays, when many people would never think of leaving their families to be with someone else's family, there is evidence that I.D. sometimes did just that for the purpose of performing ministerial duties. In short, nothing stood for long in the way of his doing his duty for God.

The reader will recall that, in an earlier chapter, the author discussed the expectations for an Old Regular Baptist minister. After much discussion, she summarized expectations for these ministers as follows: (1) They must practice the virtues that they preach to others; (2) They must study their Bibles and meditate upon Biblical verses that they've read; and (3) They must spend their lives, no matter the personal cost, ministering freely to others and doing whatever they can do, using the talents that God has given them, to lead lost sinners unto repentance.

Did I.D. Back meet these expectations? There is evidence that he, not only met but, exceeded these expectations. Did he meet the expectation that he would preach until such point that failing health or death prevented him from doing so? He did. He fulfilled ministerial duties even when he was sick himself, and he never stopped performing his duty until the day of his death. Perhaps even more importantly than exceeding the expectations for an Old Regular Baptist minister, he fulfilled the requirements of being a Christian. He repented of his sins, and asked God to forgive him for all of the wrong that he had done in his life. He obtained salvation, and, from that point on, he worked diligently to be a faithful servant to God. Because of these things, he will reap his just reward.

Since the time of I.D.'s death, his family has suffered much heartbreak. In April 2005, I.D.'s youngest son, Tony, lost his life. Less than two weeks after Tony's death, on April 19, 2005, I.D.'s grandson, Ikey Back, was involved in a fatal car crash.

Much joy, however, has also engulfed the Back family in the years following I.D.'s demise. On December 31, 2004, a new great-granddaughter (Allison Back) was born. Shortly after the deaths of Tony and Ikey Back, I.D.'s son (Ronnie) and grandson (Byron) gave their lives to God and were baptized into I.D.'s beloved Mount Olivet Old Regular Baptist Church.

At this point, however, he neither cries nor rejoices with his family. While the deaths of his loved ones would have devastated him had he been alive to witness them, the pain of these events do not impact him in his new abode.

His body now rests in a family cemetery that is located along the River Road, close to the home where he was born and raised. All senses are gone. No pain is experienced, and no joy is experienced. The body simply rests and, over time, will return to the dust from whence it came.

His spirit, however, now abides in a land where there is no sense of pain, but there is a continuous sense of joy. In his new home, he will never have to visit another sick person or preach another funeral. He will never have to endure any aches and pains, and he will never have to watch those who are close to him suffer aches and pains. He will never know the pain of losing a loved one. He will never worry about the well-being of his children, grandchildren, and great-grandchildren. No more trials and tribulations await I.D. Back.

A man of honor during his years on earth, I.D. served his country well during World War II. He was a soldier devoted to the cause of defending freedom. Since the early 1950s, however, he has fought for a greater Cause. He has been a soldier in God's army. He was a good and faithful soldier, and he fulfilled his duties well. Now, he's receiving his reward. Words from 2nd Timothy (4:6-8) seem especially fitting for I.D. Back at the time of his death. These words read as follows, "…the time of my departure is at hand. I have fought a good fight, I have finished the course, I have kept the faith. Henceforth, there is laid up for me a crown of righteousness, which the Lord, the righteous judge, shall give me at that day…."

As he said in the last journal entry recorded in the previous chapter, "I am home at last. Thank God."

BIBLIOGRAPHY

Books:

<u>A Back Family History: The Story of a Major Branch of the Back/Bach Family (Volumes 1 and 2)</u>; Kenneth Custer, Troy Back, and Dexter Dixon; copyright 1994 by the Back/Bach Genealogy Society; printed by BookCrafters

Documents:
Commonwealth of Kentucky Marriage License; #299
I.D. Back's personal journal entries

Interviews:
Adams, Ellis and Ila
Amburgey, Ivan and Mae
Asher, Phyllis
Back, I.D.
Back, Ray and Beulah
Back, Hester
Back, Ronnie
Brown, Irene
Cornett, Elwood and Kathy
Dixon, Danny and Teresa
Fugate, Callie
Fugate, Sherry
Hampton, Cliff
Preece, Wilma
Whitaker, Keller

(The author was also given access by Ronnie Back to a taped interview that Ina Rose's great-niece, Samantha Oaks, had conducted with I.D. Back. The date of the interview was February 2, 1997.)

Newspapers:
The Mountain Eagle

Web Sites:
http://www.bartleby.com
(Web site was viewed on July 10, 2003. Information obtained by the author had been taken from The Columbia Gazetteer of North America. Copyright @ 2000 Columbia University Press)

www.ingramcontent.com/pod-product-compliance
Lightning Source LLC
Chambersburg PA
CBHW022059160426
43198CB00008B/291